A GUIDE TO
THE CHILTERNS,
MARLBOROUGH DOWNS
AND OXFORD

A GUIDE TO THE CHILTERNS, MARLBOROUGH DOWNS AND OXFORD

Richard Sale

The Crowood Press

First published in 1999 by
The Crowood Press Ltd
Ramsbury, Marlborough
Wiltshire SN8 2HR

British Library Cataloguing in Publication Data
A catalogue record for this book is available from the
British Library.

ISBN 1 86126 204 3

Photograph on page 1: Exeter College, Oxford.
Photograph previous page: Near the Wantage Memorial
                              on the Berkshire Downs.

All photographs by the author except:
Pages 15, 38 and 39   Ken Hathaway
Page 81 and 187   The National Trust
Page 226   Whipsnade Wildlife Park

Typefaces used: Times New Roman (text);
                    Franklin Gothic (captions and tables).

Typeset and designed by
Carreg Limited
Hildersley, Ross-on-Wye
Herefordshire.

Printed and bound by Leo Paper Products, China.

Contents

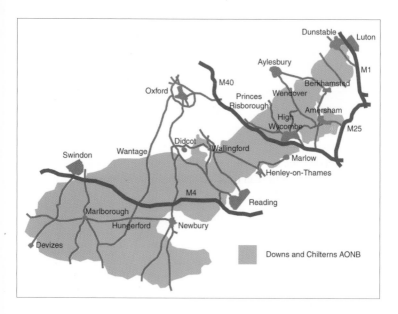

Key to Maps

———	Rivers	*A*	Art/Crafts
▬▬▬	Motorways	*M*	Museums
———	A Roads	🦉	Wildlife
———	B Roads	♣	Parks/Gardens
———	Minor roads	■	Historical Buildings
⬤ ・	Towns/villages	𝍔	Archaeological site
P	Picnic sites	✳	Other

Introduction

From Avebury, the prehistoric 'capital' of England, a band of chalk downland sweeps north-eastward across southern England. Never reaching the 1,000ft contour (about 305m), the downland does not acquire the status of a mountain. Neither is it angular or rugged in the way that mountains are. Yet it dominates the landscape, forming a high scarp on its northern side and creating a rolling landscape that is as beautiful as any mountain scene.

The downland is cut through by the Thames at the Goring Gap, which takes the river through the chalk and divides the area into two distinct sections. To the south-west are the downs of Wiltshire and Berkshire, the former more usually named for Marlborough, the town that nestles in the downland folds. Apart from the Savernake Forest, the downland here has been stripped of its tree-cover, making it a different landscape to the upland on the other side of the Thames. There, the chalk forms the Chiltern Hills where remnants of the ancient oak woods that once cloaked the chalk still thrive and where beech woods (the beech probably largely planted a few centuries ago to support the charcoal and furniture industries) are now such a feature of the landscape.

The two areas are different in ways other than the tree-cover. At the edge of the south-western downs is the most complex collection of prehistoric sites and tombs in Britain, implying that here our ancestors first cleared the downland trees, for ritual and also for agriculture. The landscape has changed little: ancient man might marvel at the size of the fields in which the crops now grow, be amazed by the farm buildings and terrified by the motorway traffic, but he would still recognize the downland, so little has the country changed over the centuries. The same can, of course, be said for the remnant woodlands of the Chilterns, but here there are more, and larger, towns crowding the old landscape. The Chilterns offer a more 'lived in' landscape. On the Downs the traveller is seeking ancient sites and solitude, and the occasional pretty village, while on the Chilterns the same traveller is seeking historical towns and imposing mansions.

Both areas have been included in an Area of Outstanding Natural Beauty (AONB) which recognizes their unique qualities and the need to preserve both the wooded and open downland. The AONB is the subject of this book, the area being explored in a series of tours from the towns likely to be used as centres by anyone visiting the area. Occasionally, an interesting site which lies just outside the AONB is visited, and one whole chapter is given over to the exploration of Oxford. Although lying outside the AONB, Oxford is so close to much of the area – just a dozen or so miles from the edge of the Berkshire Downs, about the same from the southern Chilterns – and so interesting that few visitors to the area will (or should) ignore it. Oxford is explored by a series of walks, as are the AONB's larger towns. Short walks are also suggested where they are needed to see the best of the scenery. Some of these walk suggestions use the Ridgeway National Trail, which follows what may be the country's oldest road, taking a line close to the chalk scarp edge from near Avebury to Ivinghoe Beacon at the northern edge of the Chilterns.

A Little Geology

Between 65 and 100 million years ago, in the Cretaceous period of geological time, a warm sea covered what is now southern England. In this sea lived oysters and other bivalves, corals and sea urchins: marine creatures whose shells or body structures were made of calcium carbonate. The bodies of these sea creatures built up in layers on the sea bed, layers which, hardened into rock, were exposed when the land was later raised above the sea. Calcium carbonate forms limestone, but in its purest form it also forms a softer, more friable, pure white rock: chalk. It should be noted, though, that geologists no longer favour such a simplistic view of chalk formation, favouring a production mechanism which involves not only the skeletal remains of higher marine creatures, but also a 'soup' of planktonic material and possibly even some direct chemical processes, so pure is the top layer of chalk.

The chalk beds cover much of southern England, though later processes have broken the beds into smaller sections or covered them with further sediments. Chalk surfaces in Dorset's Purbeck and in the Isle of Wight; it is seen in the South and North Downs, on the Dorset Downs and on Salisbury Plain. And it forms a narrow band that runs diagonally across the country from Wiltshire to East Anglia's northern coast. In its south-western and central sections this chalk band forms the Marlborough Downs, the Berkshire Downs and the Chilterns.

Spring in the Chilterns

The uplifting process of the chalk beds was not symmetric. It created a stepped edge (an escarpment or scarp slope) on the northern side with the land falling gently away southwards (the dip slope). As soon as the chalk had been exposed, natural processes of erosion – wind and rain, frost and ice – weathered its surface. The permeability of the chalk meant that surface rivers did not form, though there are sculpted valleys; it is conjectured that local ice sheets may have created lakes whose run-off created these valleys, but the exact method of their creation is not well understood. Most of these valleys are short, but there are two exceptions. To the south of the Marlborough Downs the Vale of Pewsey, a belt of lower, older rock, separates the Marlborough Downs from Salisbury Plain. The Vale is too wide and the River Avon apparently too insignificant for the river to have been the cause of the erosion: perhaps ice came this way. Ice is also the favoured erosion method for the Goring Gap which separates the Downs from the Chilterns, a gap through which the Thames now flows.

The chalk layer is quite thin, never more than 200m (660ft) thick, yet it is made of three quite distinct bands, prosaically called the upper, middle and lower chalk. The difference is in the amount of clay contained within the chalk. In the lower beds this can be as high as 50 per cent and creates an imperious layer. Water draining down through the middle and upper beds stops at the 'damp proof membrane' of this lower chalk and flows to the exposed surface where it emerges as springs. The middle chalk has 5–10 per cent clay and the upper chalk is the purest with virtually no clay.

Within the chalk are nodules of flint, an extremely hard, silicon-based rock with an almost vitreous lustre. The process of flint formation is not well understood, but it appears to have been formed from silica-rich organisms such as sponges, which gave up their silicon in solution, the silica then being re-deposited after the water percolated through the chalk. This sounds reasonable, but why the re-deposition should be at discrete points and why the resulting flint should be so hard and insoluble is not understood. Whatever the process, the result was the formation of lumps of virtually pure SiO_2 (flint) in a matrix of equally pure $CaCO_3$ (calcium carbonate), the pure, hard rock being much sought after by our stone-using ancestors.

A Little History

The history of man in Britain stretches back millennia before the Neolithic (New Stone Age) period, but it is a sketchy history, Palaeolithic (Old Stone Age) man leaving few signs of his presence or passage. Only in the Neolithic age did man start to leave a tangible reminder of his presence on the landscape, burying his dead in boxes of huge stones and earthing them over to form long barrows. Yet it is likely that before the Neolithic era there was already a pathway along the chalk scarp edge. The valleys and plains of early man's England were a frightening place, full of

Wayland's Smithy

Crofton Beam Engine

dense, tangled forests in which dangerous animals roamed. The chalk downs were also wooded, but the poor, dry chalk soil supported a thinner forest, one that could be traversed more easily and was less threatening. It is possible, therefore, that the ridge path was used before the Neolithic era, that is before 4,000BC. It was certainly in use after that time as the long barrows beside it and the fact that it links the flint mines of Grime's Graves to the south with the East Anglian coasts clearly show.

The period covered by the New Stone Age and the early Bronze Age is occasionally called the Megalithic era because it was then that great stone circles, stone avenues and standing stones were erected. The period also saw the construction of the most impressive long barrows, with huge stone slabs manoeuvred to form complex above-ground burial sites with chambers and linking passages, and imposing façades. At this time the Marlborough Downs were the most important place in England, the sarsen stones that littered the downs being used to create the Avebury complex, the most extraordinary collection of megalithic sites in Europe. Here there are a vast stone circle encompassing other smaller circles, an avenue of standing stones linking the circle to another ritual site, a separate ritual site on Windmill Hill, the enigma of the Silbury mound and arguably the most impressive of all long barrows. There are other sites close by, linked by the scarp edge (Ridgeway) path, while the smaller, though more famous and visually attractive, Stonehenge site is just a short distance to the south.

The Neolithic dwellers who began these monuments felled the trees which clothed the downs, clearing the land for agriculture, their domesticated animals preventing the woods from regenerating by close-cropping the downland grass. The process continues to this day, with sheep and the more recently introduced rabbit

11

now keeping the grass short and the trees at bay. In that sense the landscape the walker on the Ridgeway sees has changed little over a period of 5,000 or more years. Early Bronze Age folk probably used the long barrows for their dead and continued to use the megalithic sites, though later Bronze Age dwellers cremated their dead and placed the ashes within round barrows. When they were replaced by iron-using peoples, the use of the stone circles seems to have ended too.

The Iron Age folk – the earliest to be graced with a specific name, the Celts – originated in eastern and central Europe and expanded north. They were a warlike people, the digging of Grim's Ditch across the chalk downs usually being ascribed to the early Iron Age and the need to separate rival kingdoms. The Celts also built hill-forts, areas enclosed by ramparts and ditches into which the local folk could retreat if an enemy threatened. There are several impressive hill-forts in the AONB, the majority on the Marlborough and Berkshire Downs. The Celts defended these forts against the Romans, though the downlands seem to have been of less interest to the Romans than the fertile plains below them. Roman roads cross the chalk and use the gaps through them – most notably to carry Watling Street through the northern Chilterns – but Roman remains are few.

When the Romans retreated the hill-forts were used again, this time in an attempt to halt the relentless westward push of the Saxons. It is highly probable that if King Arthur really existed he was a Celtic warrior chief and that he fought decisive battles on, or below, the Berkshire Downs. Ultimately the Saxons were successful in taking the country, pushing the Celts into Wales and Cornwall. The Saxons later faced their own threat and on the Berkshire Downs the Saxon King Alfred fought the Danes as they attempted to move south. When the Normans came in 1066 they accepted the Saxon surrender at Berkhamsted in the Chilterns and the castle they built there remained important for centuries. The Chiltern forests, ideal hunting country and within easy reach of London, were popular with successive monarchs, including Henry VIII. The defining moment of Henry's reign was played out in the Chilterns, Thomas Cranmer choosing Dunstable Priory for the proclamation of the annulment of the King's marriage to Catherine of Aragon.

The Norman conquest had brought greater stability and peace, allowing the development of villages and towns. The wonderful village churches that characterize the area (as they do the rest of England) have their origins in late Saxon/early Norman times, as do the monasteries, the great manor houses and the earliest Oxford colleges. The growth

Wyld Court Rainforest Conservation Centre

of Oxford was the most spectacular in the area until the Industrial Revolution, its importance making it an obvious choice for King Charles I when he was seeking a capital from which to wage the Civil War against Parliament's forces. Important battles were fought at Newbury as the opposing sides vied for control of the routes to London.

With the Restoration and settled times the towns of the area became important coaching stops on routes to and from London. Marlborough was on the way to Bath, while the towns of the Chiltern gaps were important stopovers on the way to Oxford and the Midland cities. It was at this time that the position of Steward of the Chiltern Hundreds became an important position. The 'hundred' is a Saxon administrative unit comprising one hundred families, and the Chilterns area is one of the few places in England where the word is still in common usage, in the Chiltern Hundreds and the Three Hundreds of Aylesbury. The Steward of the Chiltern Hundreds was charged with protecting travellers from highwaymen. It was an important position in its time, and

Kennet and Avon Canal

Chequers from the Ridgeway

Walford Church

though no longer a real position it is still part of the British Parliamentary system: if an MP wishes to resign he does so by applying for the post of Steward. Technically the Stewardship is an official, paid position and the MP is not, therefore, allowed to hold it.

The industrialization of Britain brought canals – the Kennet and Avon through the Vale of Pewsey to Newbury and a branch of the Grand Union to Wendover – and then railways, but the lack of mineral wealth prevented full-scale industrial development in the area. The Marlborough and Berkshire Downs had already lost their woodland, but there were sufficient areas left on the Chilterns for charcoal burning and then furniture making (particularly chair making at High Wycombe) to be important. It is likely that during this time beech woods were planted as well as cut down, the beech woods that are such a spectacular feature of the area perhaps dating from this time. The Chilterns also gained from their closeness to London, merchants and politicians escaping the city to build great houses and increase the prosperity of local towns. Eventually the value of the Chiltern woodlands to city dwellers needing a little respite from the stresses of modern life led to the creation of the Area of Outstanding Natural Beauty, the AONB rightly extending to the southern downlands, England's most ancient man-made landscape.

(Opposite) The Marlborough Downs near Liddington Castle

Marlborough and the Western Downs

Marlborough

The town for which the western part of the high chalk downland is named – the Ordnance Survey applies Marborough's name only to the downs lying north of the town, but the locals also tend to apply it to those to the south – is quite charming. Some disparagingly say it consists of just one long street. Well, so it does – but what a spectacular street.

The town's name derives from the Saxon *Merle Beorg*, Merlin's Grave. The 'grave' was the mound at the western end of the town, in what are now the grounds of Marlborough College. In Norman times this mound was topped by a castle of typical 'motte and bailey' form, but as the Celtic origin of the name proves, the motte (mound) existed before the Norman conquest. Excavations show that the mound pre-dated the Celts too, being a contemporary of Silbury Hill which lies to the west, towards Avebury. The Celtic name for the mound is no surprise, the Celts often linking mythical or legendary heroes with features they did not understand, but the idea that Merlin could lie beneath a mound on the Marlborough Downs is an intriguing link with a real Arthur for, as we shall see, the famous Battle of Badon might have taken place on the downs.

A modification of the old name created the 'borough': perhaps this occurred after the town had been granted a charter by King John in 1204. But the town did not forget its link with Arthur's magician, adopting the motto *Ubi Nunc Sapientis Ossa Merlini* – 'Where lie the bones of the wise Merlin.'

The Saxon village of Marlborough was sited on what is now The Green, at the eastern end of the town. The Normans used the mound at what is now the western end, the medieval development of the town linking the two with what is claimed to be the widest high street in Britain. To explore the town we shall start at The Green.

Medieval towns and villages, with their timber-framed, thatched houses were plagued by fire, the limited firefighting techniques and equipment of the age occasionally allowing fires to spread, with disastrous consequences. Marlborough was no

The Green, Marlborough

exception, a fire in 1653 destroying around 250 houses, a large part of the town, and causing enough damage to so impoverish the townsfolk that a subscription was taken up throughout England to enable rebuilding to start. Further fires in 1679 and 1690 were less disastrous, but so fearful did the town council become that following the latter blaze a byelaw was passed forbidding the use of thatch as a roofing material. Many of the houses at The Green date from the rebuilding after the 1653 fire, though it is claimed that the cellars in some actually date from the town's Saxon period.

Facing the church, Barn Street goes left to New Road where Christchurch, a Methodist/United Reformed Church dating from 1910, is the latest of several Methodist churches on the site: John Wesley is known to have preached in the town several times in the 1740s. To the right of The Green is Silverless Street with several very attractive houses. Look, especially, at Nos 13 and 15, two small timbered cottages dating from soon after the 1653 fire and so retaining the medieval-style overhanging upper storeys. The avenue of lime trees on the far side of The Green was planted in 1840. Beyond it is Patten Alley, so called because it was necessary to wear pattens – a shoe or clog, usually set on an iron ring – when taking it on muddy days. A plaque on No. 29, to the right, notes that it was where William Golding, author of *Lord of the Flies* and other fine novels, and winner of the 1983 Nobel Prize for Literature, spent his boyhood: his father taught at the local grammar school, where Golding was educated before going up to Brasenose College, Oxford.

Follow the alley to reach St Mary's Church. The church dates from the mid-12th century, but little is Norman, most now dating from a 15th century rebuild. In the fire of 1653 St Mary's was gutted and the reddening of the internal stonework is still visible – look, particularly, at the west wall. As you leave the church, look above the porch to the left to see some carvings – now very weathered – of cats. A local legend maintains that this commemorates a cat who repeatedly returned to the church tower to rescue her kittens during the 1653 fire. It is a lovely story, but the carvings actually date from the 15th century rebuild. Continue along Patten Alley then bear left to reach the High Street, with the Town Hall, built in fine style in 1900, to the left. The High Street is a delight, its looks spoiled only by the central car park and the cars lining its pavement. A little way along, to the right (No. 132), the Merchant's House dates from 1656 (immediately post-fire). It was built for a goldsmith who clearly spared no expense. Inside, the 'Great Parlour' has original full-length oak wall panelling, while elsewhere there is more original decoration. This fine house is now being turned into a museum of late 17th century town life.

The High Street has some fine buildings, several of which were coaching inns, Marlborough being on the coach route from Bath to London. The Ivy House Hotel is claimed to be the best building in town, with the Merlin Hotel laying a claim to being the most historically important. Here (or, rather, in a building on the same site) one of Henry III's parliaments was held in the days when there was no permanent home for it, its members following the King's progress around the country. Some historians claim that as the King stayed at the castle the parliament is more likely to have been held there, but tradition argues for the Merlin.

A plaque about half way along the High Street (on the northern side) recalls the Civil War skirmish when a Royalist band broke into the town. Marlborough's council was for Parliament (though many locals were Royalists) and there were a few Parliamentarian troops in the town. The Royalists were resisted for some time, eventually fighting their way to the High Street through narrow side alleys. The mayor and council were then force-marched through the snow to the Royalist HQ at Oxford. The nearby plaques recall visits to the town by Samuel Pepys, the famous diarist, and the Lord Chamberlain's men. The latter were a 16th century group of travelling actors who included William Shakespeare among their number. The men apparently made four visits to the town, though it is not certain that the Great Man was with them on any of these occasions.

Marlborough Town Hall

Opposite the plaques, a modern arch leads to The Priory, a fine early 19th century house overlooking public gardens beside the River Kennet. The house, which stands on the site of a 14th century monastery, has been converted into sheltered housing.

At the bottom of the High Street, on the left, another plaque marks the spot where the great fire of 1653 began, at the tanning shop of Francis Freeman. Oak bark, used in the tanning process, caught fire, and within three hours the flames, fanned by a strong wind, had virtually destroyed the town. Further on, standing on an island in the wide street is the church of St Peter and St Paul, built in the 15th century but remodelled later. Standing to the west of Francis Freeman's shop, and with the wind from the south-west, the church (and the nearby buildings) survived the 1653 fire. Inside is a sad memorial to the three young children of Sir Nicholas Hyde who all died in a short time in early 1626, presumably of a contagious disease. It is a poignant reminder of the fragility of medieval life.

Beyond the church is Marlborough College. As noted above, the Neolithic mound became the motte of a Norman castle in the 11th century, though this was in ruins by the 16th century. At that time Sir Francis Seymour built a house below the mound. This was replaced in the 17th century by the Duke of Somerset who landscaped the mound, adding hanging gardens and a grotto. The latter remains, but the trees which now shroud the mound have destroyed what remained of the gardens. Over the next hundred years the house was gradually extended, and further buildings were added. Then, in 1750, on the death of seventh Duke of Somerset, the house became vacant and was let as a coaching inn, without doubt the grandest in the town. The Castle Inn remained open until 1843 when the site became a college for 200

A quiet corner of Marlborough

boys. It remains a public school, and is not open to the public.

From St Peter's Church, walk back along High Street, turn right through the arch to The Priory and walk through the gardens to the bridge over the Kennet. Cross and turn left, going through the car park by the Tourist Information Centre and following the road to re-cross the Kennet. At this point there was once a mill, its water-wheel driven by the river, owned by John Churchill, the general whose victory at Blenheim in 1704 over the army of Louis XIV saved Europe from French expansionism. A grateful nation gave Churchill the money to build Blenheim Palace near Oxford. John Churchill's father was Sir Winston: one of the later members of the family was a more famous Sir Winston Churchill. John Churchill took the title first Duke of Marlborough, in part because of his holdings here which had been inherited from his mother, who came from a (defunct) line of Earls of Marlborough.

The road across the Kennet bridge soon rejoins the High Street.

Marlborough High Street

TOUR 1: The Northern Downs and the Ridgeway

Our first tour explores the Downs to the north of Marlborough, those crossed by the Ridgeway, said to be Europe's oldest road.

It is often claimed that the **Ridgeway**, the track that crosses the high chalk downland of Wiltshire and Berkshire, staying close to the down's northern edge, is Europe's oldest road. That is, of course, debatable as there is limited hard evidence for its use before the coming of the Saxons (who named it *hrycg*, that being Saxon for 'ridge'). Palaeolithic (Old Stone Age) hand axes have been found near Marlborough, tempting some historians to claim that even before the last Ice Age – more than 12,000 years ago – folk were using the route. Though conjecture, this claim is not unreasonable: the Britain of that time, still attached to mainland Europe by a land bridge, was a dangerous place, the valleys filled with dense forest in which man was not only the hunter but the hunted, and the less well-covered chalk ridge would have been a comparatively safe route. Neolithic (New Stone Age) folk almost certainly used the road, their burial chambers being found close to it. Then, as now, people put their temples and cemeteries near the road. The Bronze Age folk also built beside the road, and the Saxons almost certainly used it as they advanced westward against the Celts. Most intriguingly, it has been suggested that Arthur, the mythical Celtic king, may have won his battles against the Saxons close to the old road.

The Ridgeway's use continued through medieval times, the route eventually becoming a 'drove' road. In the days before refrigeration, animals were brought to town on the hoof for slaughter and immediate sale. The herds were controlled by men employed specifically for the task, the drovers, who used ancient tracks to avoid the rutted muddy trails that most roads of the time were, and to stay close to free fodder for the herds. A drove would have been a fine sight for not only were cattle, sheep and pigs herded, but chickens, geese and turkeys too. The poultry had their

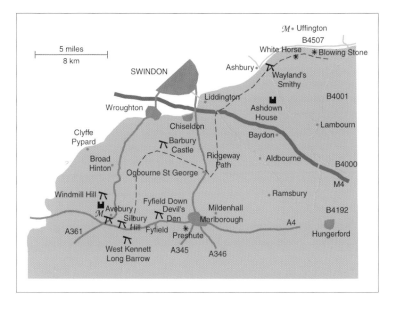

feet encased in pitch to withstand the rigours of the journey, and bulls were shod to save their hooves from cracking under their weight: it is said (and easily believed) that the men who shod the bulls were both brave and skilled, and earned every penny of their fee.

The drovers used a collection of parallel tracks on the high downs, but the Enclosures Act forced the definition of a single route. It is that route which the National Trail (as official long-distance footpaths are now termed) now follows. It is wonderful when following that route to contemplate the fact that your feet are following a route that your ancestors trod several thousand years ago.

Technically the Ridgeway is a road and can be driven along much of its length, no matter how unreasonable such a use might seem. It occasionally is driven too, by four-wheel drive vehicles and motorcycles, though a series of voluntary bans means that for most of the time it is left to walkers, horse-riders and mountain bikers. The best of the ancient features along the way are easily reached from well-sited car parks, but the sections of country between these features – the high down with its long views – are one of the Ridgeway's joys. Short walks from the features are therefore worthwhile. The use of two cars or public transport to allow longer sections of the route (which is entirely linear, though circular walks can be created) is better. Best, of course, is to follow the path: the section from the start, near Avebury, to Streatley, passing the finest ancient sites, is 67km (42 miles) long.

From Marlborough head west (towards Avebury and Calne) along the A4, soon passing a turn on the left for **Preshute**, where St George's Church has its origins in the 12th century, but is now largely mid-19th century. Behind the church is Preshute House, dating from the early 19th century and now part of Marlborough College, while on the hill to the south is a white horse, the first of several we shall see on this western edge of the downs. This one – the best approach is from the A345 (Salisbury) road, just south of Marlborough – was cut in 1804 by boys from Marlborough School. (It is often claimed that the horse was cut by pupils of

The Ridgeway

Marlborough College, but this is not so as the figure pre-dates the college by forty years.) The figure is actually a very good representation of a horse, but is difficult to see as the ground on which it is cut is at a shallow angle and from what would be the best vantage points it tends to be obscured by trees and hedges.

The A4 now follows the River Kennet closely, with occasional fine views of the downs to the right. **Fyfield**, the next village, has a name famous to archaeologists, Fyfield Down, to the north, being renowned for its sarsen stones. The village is therefore usually used as little more than a starting point for an exploration of the down, which is sad as it is better than that: look for the tiny flint-built church, probably dating from the 13th century though much remodelled. There are also several pleasant houses.

The chalk of the Marlborough and Berkshire Downs was laid down beneath a calm sea – chalk being no more than a very fine-grained, soft limestone – during the Cretaceous period. During later eras the chalk was covered with a thin layer of a hard sandstone. Sandstone is, as the name implies, created from sand, a desert then existing where a clear sea had previously washed. Sand is converted into rock by a process known as diagenesis in which some form of cement glues the sand grains together. Subsequent earth movements broke the thin sandstone layer into slabs of various sizes, littering **Fyfield Down** with blocks of stone. It was these blocks which the megalithic (meaning, literally, 'large stone') builders used to create their monuments. The blocks are known as sarsens, though the origin of the word is not well understood: many believe it derives from 'Saracen' as the monuments were seen as being of pagan (i.e. non-Christian) origin in medieval times. The local name for the blocks is 'grey wethers', meaning grey sheep, as from a distance the blocks are hard to distinguish from grazing sheep.

The sarsens of Fyfield Down were hauled to Avebury and Stonehenge as well as to smaller local sites, but Fyfield was more than a surface quarry for megaliths. At OS grid reference 152697 – reached by following the lane north to, and beyond, Fyfield Hill Farm, then bearing right along a footpath – the **Devil's Den** is a dolmen or cromlech. Neolithic man buried his dead (the important ones at least) in a 'box' of stone slabs which was then earthed over to form a long barrow. Occasionally time has eroded the earth mound, revealing the stone box which stands, enigmatically, against the elements. To later folk, who had lost the knowledge of how to raise vast blocks of stone, those monuments seemed supernatural – hence the name. In comparison to the elaborate long barrows closer to Avebury, the Devil's Den is a modest structure, perhaps one of the earliest to have been built. Fyfield Down also shows evidence of post-megalithic use, Iron Age (Celtic) and Roman field systems being present and a Saxon track (Herapath or Green Street) running along the northern edge of these systems. The name 'herapath' is interesting: it means 'army track'; this is the way the Saxons came on their westward push.

Fyfield Down is crossed by several paths which allow an exploration of the ancient landscape. The Down is now a National Nature Reserve to preserve both the stones and the wildlife, and a particularly fine section (Piggle Dene, just west of Fyfield village) is owned by the National Trail: to preserve the landscape please keep to the marked footpaths.

West again, the A4 rejoins the Kennet (which performed a southerly loop away from Fyfield). The road follows the line of a Roman road linking Bath to *Cunetio*, their settlement near Marlborough (*see* page 47) and on eastwards, but just before turning to the left for the village of West Overton, the older road takes a straight line to the right, a line still visible on the ground. The road now climbs gently up Overton Hill to the start of the Ridgeway.

There is a car park at the route's start: immediately across the road from the start is **The Sanctuary**. Today all that can be seen at The Sanctuary is a series of concrete posts which mark the position of concentric circles of wooden posts and standing stones. Archaeologists believe the posts and stones represent three phases of building, starting in about 3,000BC and ending in about 2,300BC, the site gradually enlarging from a simple conical roofed hut to a much larger, but still roofed, structure which incorporated a stone circle. As with all the megalithic sites, the true nature of the huts is not – and perhaps will never be – known, but excavations have led to a widely accepted theory. The name was given to the site by William Stukeley, a famous early 18th century antiquarian, and though his theory was pure conjecture, it may not have been far off the truth. Overton Hill is a prominent local feature and it is likely to have been for that reason that the first hut was built on its summit. Perhaps a priest or shaman lived there. Excavations show evidence of burials and feasting: probably the bodies of the dead were laid out in a 'sky burial', with birds and animals picking the bones clean for later burial, interment perhaps accompanied by feasting. The famous avenue of standing stones from Avebury ended at The Sanctuary: as there is no evidence of burials at Avebury, it is likely that burials were preceded by rituals there, perhaps with a procession between the two.

Avebury is our next objective too: continue along the A4 to West Kennett – we shall explore the West Kennett Long Barrow later – turning right there to reach the village along a road which runs parallel with the great stone avenue. Most visitors have come to see the great megalithic site, but the village is also worth a short tour. The main village car park lies to the south; if arriving along the stone avenue, turn left along the A4361, then right into the car park from where a footpath reaches the stone circle near its southwestern sector. Turn left along High Street, then right to reach the National Trust Shop – the Trust owns the Avebury site, the stone avenue and other local parcels of land, including Windmill Hill – and the Great Barn complex. The barn, once known as the Parson's Barn, is a magnificent 17th century thatched tithe barn and is now the centrepiece of a rural life museum exploring Wiltshire life in the late 19th/early 20th centuries. Of the local exhibits the most interesting is the rope-making machine of Samuel Pratt. This was

Sarsen stones, Fyfield Down

set up near the United Reform Church at the eastern end of the village with ropes being laid out along Green Street (*see* above). The museum also has a life-size photo of Fred Kempster who lived in the village in the early 20th century and who was 2.54m (8ft 4in – exactly 100 inches) tall. The village's Tourist Information Office is within the Great Barn complex.

Close to the Great Barn is St James' Church. The first church on the site was Saxon and parts of this still remain (three small round windows on the north nave wall), but it was incorporated into a Norman building which was expanded several times, most recently in the 16th century. The font is Saxon, but the plain Saxon cylinder was decorated with carvings in early Norman times. Across from the church is the Alexander Keiller Museum which houses the best finds excavated from Windmill Hill and the other local sites.

Just beyond the museum is Avebury Manor, built on the site of the Benedictine Priory founded in the 12th century but dissolved in the early 15th. The museum is actually housed in the coach house and stables of the manor which was begun in the mid-16th century, using stone from the priory and from the breaking up of standing stones from the megalithic sites. The house was extended in Queen Anne style, then renovated in Edwardian style by a Colonel Jenner, who also laid out formal gardens. In the 1930s Alexander Keiller, the leader of the team of excavators on Windmill Hill and the man responsible for re-erecting some of the Avebury stones, bought the manor, making it the centre of his Morven Institute for archaeological research. It is known that John Aubrey and William Stukeley both stayed at the house, so it has a proud place in the history of the unravelling of Avebury's secrets. It is also claimed that Queen Anne dined here. When Keiller sold his Avebury lands in 1942 the National Trust could not afford the manor, which remained in private hands until the Trust finally acquired it in the late 1980s. A long and thorough period of restoration followed: at first only the gardens with their topiary and flower beds were open, but now the house can be visited as well.

To complete a short tour of Avebury village, go through the churchyard – note the thatched churchyard wall on the right – to regain High Street and turn left.

In 1663 King Charles II was travelling to Bath with the antiquarian John Aubrey and the two decided to make a short detour to see the megalithic site which, even then, was famous. Aubrey was impressed. 'It does as much exceed in greatness the so renowned Stonehenge', he wrote 'as a cathedral doth a parish church.' For many visitors the initial reaction is that Avebury is less impressive than Stonehenge, but after a walk around and a contemplation of its complexity and size, many reconsider and agree with Aubrey. When complete the main Avebury monument covered over 28 acres, was circled by a ditch 350m (1,140ft) in diameter that was up to 9m (30ft) deep, and a bank 1,350m (4,500ft) long and almost 7m (nearly 20ft) high. Inside were around 250 standing stones, the tallest over 7m high, some weighing over 60 tons. This complex was linked by an avenue of a hundred pairs of standing stones to The Sanctuary almost 2km (1$\frac{1}{4}$miles) away and (probably) another avenue heading towards Beckhampton. The sheer engineering effort is breathtaking and is estimated to have taken over 1$\frac{1}{2}$ million man-hours, at a time when the local population was probably numbered in thousands.

The Stone Circle, Avebury

Avebury was not constructed in one vast effort. It is believed that the outer ditch was dug in about 2700BC, after the first phase of The Sanctuary (and also the completion of the first stage of Stonehenge) and completed by about 2300BC, perhaps 200 years before Stonehenge's final phases. When completed the site comprised a roughly circular ditch/bank pierced by four entrance-ways. The actual shape is sufficiently irregular to suggest that for all their undoubted engineering sophistication the builders did not have very accurate surveying methods and that the construction was piecemeal, with gangs of diggers working towards each other and sometimes not meeting as they might have hoped. The four entrances now carry the main road and Avebury High Street.

Just within the ditch was a circle of ninety-eight standing stones, of which only thirty remain (and three of these have fallen and not been re-erected). Within this circle there were two further stone circles, each of which had a further feature at its centre. These two smaller circles have few of the thirty or so stones they originally comprised. At the centre of the northern circle is what Stukeley called The Cove, a collection of at least three upright stones forming a row which appears to be aligned to the moon's most northerly point of rising. At the centre of the southern circle is the more complex 'Z feature'. Stukeley records that at the heart of this was a stone (fallen even in his day) which, when standing, would have been well over 6m (more than 21ft) tall and almost 3m (9ft) in diameter. This stone, which Stukeley called the Obelisk, was broken up for building stone a few years after he sketched it.

The loss of stones is due, in large part, to their destruction in medieval times. Stukeley records that periodically pits were dug beneath the stones and filled with straw, which was then burned. The heated stone was then doused with cold water, after which it could be easily broken up with hammers. This has often been portrayed as a Christian ritual, the church supervising the symbolic destruction of a pagan emblem. In fact it was merely the easy production of building stone for the expanding village of Avebury. The legend of a church ritual probably derives from the discovery that many of the stones had been dropped and buried in earlier times in what was certainly an attempt to deprive the site of its power. That so many stones survive is due to this earlier burying and to the efforts of Alexander Keiller – the marmalade heir and amateur (but very good) archaeologist – who bought the site in 1930 and re-erected the excavated stones. During the raising of Stone 9 (the sixth stone from either end of the south-west sector of the outer stone circle) the remains of a man were found. Coins found on the man dated his death to about 1320 and it is assumed that he was part of a team dropping and burying the stone, and was crushed when it fell. No attempt had been made to extract his body for burial. Other finds on the skeletal remains suggest the man was an itinerant barber-surgeon; perhaps he was in Avebury for just a day or two, and joined in for the fun of it – fun, that is, until the stone fell.

A walk around the outer stone circle is very worthwhile, just to gauge the size of the site and the stones. The so-called Portal Stones (Stones 1 and 98, to the right of the road as you reach the site from The Sanctuary) are each 4m (14ft) high and must have formed an impressive entranceway. As with the Devil's Den on Fyfield Down, the pair attracted a superstitious name, the Devil's Chair. At the opposite side of the circle, Stone 46 (called the Swindon Stone as it lies beside the road to Swindon) is estimated to be the site's heaviest, at about 65 tons.

William Stukeley drew a map of Avebury and the nearby sites in 1743 showing two avenues, one leading to The Sanctuary, the other towards Beckhampton. Stukeley contrived to make the combination look like a snake; he also 'adjusted' his measurements and the stone positions to fit his own view of the sites, which he believed were druidic in origin. In fact, the druids post-date Avebury by at least 2,000 years, perhaps a few centuries more. **West Kennett Avenue**, leading to The Sanctuary, is clearly visible, but the Beckhampton avenue is more speculative. The West Kennett Avenue comprised about a hundred pairs of stones. These, as with the main Avebury sites but unlike Stonehenge, were not dressed, but erected as found. Some have seen a regular pattern of triangular and phallic shapes in the stones and gone on to speculate a fertility rite basis for the avenue's existence, but others are less convinced.

To the south of Avebury, lying beside the A4 to the west of West Kennett is **Silbury Hill**, the most enigmatic of the ancient sites. The hill is the largest man-made mound in Europe and is as large as the smaller of Egypt's great pyramids. A tunnel dug into the centre of the hill has revealed that the mound was constructed in three phases, the first in about 2700BC, the last about 400 years later. It is ironical that science can tell us that the first phase – the building of a mound about 36m (120ft) in diameter, $4^{1}/_{2}$m (15ft) high – started in late summer (probably August) because winged ants were trapped in the cut turfs, but can tell us nothing about why it was built. The second mound was conical, but the final mound was similar to the step pyramid, with circular retaining walls rising from flat shelves. The shelves were then infilled with soil to create a smooth cone with a face angle of 60 degrees, though the top was left flat. The mound is 40m (130ft) high and 160m (525ft) in diameter. It covers five acres and required the moving of about 400,000cu m (14 million cubic feet) of chalk. Given the statistics the mound was clearly very important, so what was it for? It lies in a valley and is not easily seen from a distance, so it was obviously not meant to make an impression on arriving travellers. It was not visible from the Avebury site when the banks

Silbury Hill

The West Kennett Avenue

were at full height. Excavations have revealed no burials, either of men, animals or treasure, so it does not appear to have been a vast tomb. It has been speculated that it marks the site of a battle, but that seems to be going to a lot of trouble – one calculation suggests that the third phase work required three million man hours, say one thousand men working ten hours per day non-stop for a year. Despite the endless speculation we are left with no better suggestion than the local legend that the mound is the tomb of (as yet undiscovered) King Sel. The legend maintains that the king was buried upright with his horse and that both wear armour of solid gold. Finally, please note that the mound cannot be climbed.

From Avebury a marvellous walk of about 11km (7 miles) – allow half a day for stops along the way – links the main mega-lithic sites. From the car park turn right, with care, along the main road for 50m, then cross and follow an enclosed path southwards. This path bears left, and circles Silbury Hill to reach the A4. Cross with care and follow the path opposite. The Wiltshire Downs are the crop circle centre of Britain (due the alien interest in the Avebury monuments, or so it is said) and there are usually good examples in the field here. Soon turn sharp left and continue along the path: a sharp right turn now detours to the West Kennett Long Barrow. The route continues eastwards, crossing a minor road and bearing right to join a bridleway. Turn left to reach a road. Cross and follow the path opposite to reach the Wessex Ridgeway Path. Turn left along this to reach The Sanctuary. Now follow the Ridgeway Trail up on to Overton Down. After 3km (about 2 miles) Green Street joins from the left: turn left and follow it to a road end, continuing along the road to return to Avebury.

West Kennett Long Barrow is one of the best preserved Neolithic tombs in Britain. It is also one of the most impressive, its entranceway closed by vast 'blocking' stones. The Devil's Den, a simple stone box, represents the basic form of Neolithic long barrow. West Kennett is far more sophisticated, a passage from the entrance having two pairs of side burial chambers and finishing in a fifth chamber. The passage and chambers are roofed with large flat slabs and the whole covered with a huge earth mound. This mound is 100m (305ft) long, second in length of British barrows only to that at East Kennett. Of this 100m, only 12m (about 40ft) is taken up by the burial passage – the rest appears to be earth alone. It is thought the tomb was constructed around 3500BC but continued in use for around 1500 years, the final sealing with the blocking stone slabs being in about 2000BC.

West Kennett Long Barrow

Excavations revealed skeletal fragments of forty-six bodies, not many for so long a use, but the way the bones were piled up and the fact that few skeletons were complete implies that periodic clearing or sorting of the bones may have taken place. When constructed, the barrow had a ditch running along each side and a forecourt in front of the entrance, presumably for rituals associated with new burials. The elaborate façade of the barrow is its most impressive feature, and was presumably of great symbolic importance, so much so that it comprises not only local sarsens, but slabs of oolitic limestone brought to the site from the Bath area.

The final site of the Avebury prehistoric complex is **Windmill Hill** which lies to the north-west of the village. This dominating hill is topped by a causeway camp, a series of three concentric ditches/banks breached by chalk causeways. The outer ditch encloses an area of twenty-one acres, making Windmill Hill the largest Neolithic camp discovered to date. The exact purpose of the enclosure is unclear. Similar sites were obviously inhabited by folk living in permanent huts, but at Windmill Hill excavations suggest seasonal occupation only, perhaps for feasting as the ditches are full of animal bones and pottery shards. But there are human bones too, suggesting that the site also had a funereal function. A square enclosure just outside the outer ditch is believed to have been the site of cremations and 'sky' burials and, after the bones had been picked clean, for rituals which culminated in some bones being put into the ditches. Quite why some bones were disposed of with household rubbish and what happened to the bones that were not thrown in the ditches is not known, but most experts now believe the rituals carried out here and at the other local sites involved some form of ancestor worship.

To continue the tour of Ridgeway sites, head north from Avebury, following the A4361, with Windmill Hill off to the left and Overton Down to the right, to reach **Winterborne Monkton**, a pretty village with a church that has an unusual shingled belfry. The first part of the name is the old local name for the stream that forms the upper reaches of the Kennet. It was a 'winterbourne', a winter stream, summer's waters often disappearing into the chalk. Further north, a left turn crosses a humpback bridge over the winterbourne to reach **Berwick Bassett**, another pretty village, one with two manor houses, the older 15th century, the other a couple of centuries newer. The next village to the north, which also lies off the main road, is also named for the winter stream. **Winterborne Bassett** is less pretty than its neighbours, but has a lovely little church: look for the memorials to the Baskerville family and the weathered 13th century effigy figures. From the village a narrow road heads north-west to **Clyffe Pypard** where the church is a much more striking building. The village is named for its position, set into a steep section of downland as it falls towards the Wiltshire plain, and for a 13th century lord, Richard Pipard. With its backing of beech-shrouded cliff, the village is wonderfully picturesque. The church dates from the 15th century, but has been drastically restored. Inside look for the pulpit, dated 1629 and beautifully decorated. The nave has an excellent wagon roof and there is a superb, life-size white marble memorial effigy of Thomas Spackman, a carpenter who died in 1786 leaving money in his will for the education of the village's poor children. Sir Nikolaus Pevsner, author of the *Buildings of Britain* series of books on county architecture, and his wife are buried in the churchyard.

Close to Clyffe Pypard are the sites of three medieval villages, built on the spring line of the chalk escarpment. It is likely that they were not resettled after Black Death had killed their inhabitants. Also abandoned was the Norman motte and bailey castle of Bincknall, built on a chalk spur overlooking Wootton Bassett. There is little to see, but it can be reached by a footpath from **Broad Hinton**, another picturesque village lying just off the main road. The church here is worth visiting for the number and quality of its monuments, these including several to members of the Wroughton family and one to a Colonel Glanville, who died for his king during the Civil War, which includes not only an alabaster effigy in full armour, but his real armour and a death figure in a shroud.

As the road from Broad Hinton to Broad Town descends the steep chalk scarp, a footpath heading north can be used to see what remains of a white horse cut by a local farmer in 1863, one of Wiltshire's least known chalk figures. A better known figure is the horse cut on the side of **Hackpen Hill**, which is crossed by a minor road opposite the turning to Broad Hinton. Though well-known, the horse is quite difficult to see as the hill slope is only 30 degrees, leading to considerable foreshortening. The figure's origins are not known, but experts favour a cutting in 1838 to celebrate the Coronation of Queen Victoria.

Clyffe Pypard Church

Back on the main road, the view eastwards (to the right) is now dominated by the northern spur of the Marlborough Downs, on the extremity of which sits Barbury Castle. That is our next destination, but to reach it we must continue to Wroughton, passing, on the right, an airfield whose large hangers are an annexe of the **Science Museum**, housing items too large to be accommodated in the museum's London home. The collection includes civil and military aircraft, missiles, buses, commercial vehicles and steam engines.

Continue into **Wroughton**, a pleasant town – the church, unusually dedicated to St John the Baptist and St Helen, has a fine Norman doorway – and follow the signs to reach the car park at **Barbury Castle**. The castle is an Iron Age hill-fort, the natural

Approaching Barbury Castle

defences of the downland slopes being reinforced by two rings of ditches and ramparts, these enclosing an area of $11^1/_2$ acres. Unlike Windmill Hill, this hill-fort was almost certainly a purely defensive structure, though there is evidence of huts inside, indicating seasonal occupation or, perhaps, a permanent garrison at some stage. The ditch and rampart, together with the natural shape, made the storming of the fort a perilous venture for an invading force. The fact that there are two ditches and ramparts points to Barbury having been built during the later Iron Age, the development of the slingshot requiring wider defences. Hill-forts were not used for permanent occupation, the local population retreating to the fort when an invading enemy threatened. Iron Age sieges were unlikely to have been very long lasting because of the difficulties of keeping an army in the field, but on chalk the defenders would have needed to solve the water problem as Barbury is built well above the spring line. The defenders could have brought water in leather buckets, but that would have taken time. It is more likely that they used dew ponds; these were large excavated depressions lined with clay to make them waterproof, the clay being mixed with soot which deterred worms and burrowing insects which might have caused leaks. The ponds were filled by rain or condensing clouds. The downland farmers continued to use this method of collecting water until electric pumps allowed valley water to be pumped to upland troughs.

Barbury's name is thought to derive from *Beran Byrg*, 'Bera's Hill', Bera perhaps being one of the leaders of the Saxon army which defeated the Celts on the slopes below the fort in AD565. (The actual Saxon chieftain at the battle was Cynric, but perhaps Bera captured the hill-fort, or held it afterwards.) The fort is now the central feature of a Country Park – there are car parks on both sides of the castle – and a walk along the ramparts is worthwhile for the view of the downs and towards Swindon. The Ridgeway National Trail crosses the castle: from the eastern car park the Trail can be followed along Smeathe's Ridge, a prominent feature offering further splendid views.

An alternative walk from the eastern car park reaches a standing stone erected as a memorial to two local writers. Richard Jeffries (1848–87) was a reporter on the *North Wilts Herald* who wrote about twenty books on the local way of life and Wiltshire characters. He is now recognized as one of the 19th century's finest writers on pastoral affairs, and his lyricism can still strike a chord today. Jeffries was born at Coate, then a village to the south-east of Swindon, now one of the town's suburbs. There is a

The Downs in autumn

small museum to him there, and a bust to his memory in Salisbury Cathedral. Alfred Williams (1877–1930), another local man, was a naturalist and gifted poet. Words from each of these fine writers are inscribed on their memorial tablets.

Return to Wroughton and follow the B4005 to **Chiseldon**, where the older cottages are made of sarsen stone and chalk. Richard Jeffries was married in Holy Cross Church, a Norman building around a Saxon core. From the village it is a short distance to the Jeffries Museum in Coate and to the railway museums of Swindon. Now cross the A345, go through Badbury and over the M4 to **Liddington**. A Roman villa was discovered here during the construction work on the motorway.

Liddington is a pretty village with some thatched cottages and a fine Jacobean manor house. The village gives its name to another Iron Age hill-fort, here with a single ditch and rampart system, which lies 2km (1$\frac{1}{4}$ miles) to the south and on the route of the Ridgeway National Trail. Some experts have suggested that the hill-fort is the Mount Badon at which King Arthur defeated the Saxons in his greatest battle against them. Nennius, a Welsh chronicler writing in about AD800, notes that Arthur, a Celtic warlord, won a series of twelve battles against the Saxons, halting their westward advance across Britain for a generation. The early

Summer Thunder Clouds over Ashdown House

battles in this series have been identified as being in the north of England, but the location of the greatest victory, at *Mons Badonicus*, is disputed. Many military historians have noted that a Saxon advance would have used rivers as the Saxons were undoubted masters of both the sea and inland waterways (in comparison with the British Celts). The Saxons would therefore have used the Thames in their westward push, and also used the ancient Ridgeway for a land-based advance. The Celts, descendants of the hillfort builders, can be expected to have used the forts for defence. It seems possible therefore that the downs were the scene of the Battle of Badon. Badbury, close to Liddington, has been suggested as the origin of Badon, as has Baydon, a village to the east (*see* below). Baydon lies on a Roman road and the remains of another fort lies close by. It has to be said, though, that Badbury Rings in Dorset (another hill-fort) has also been suggested as a location for Badon, and there is no shortage of other suggestions.

The Saxons were a patient enemy. After the defeats inflicted by Arthur they merely put down their swords and waited. Arthur seems to have been active in about AD500. By 565 the Saxons had been victorious at Barbury Castle: they had picked up their swords and moved west once more. In 577 at Dyrham, to the east of Bristol, they won a decisive battle, reaching the Severn and splitting the Britons in two (those in Wales, and those in the southwest, who were eventually pushed all the way to Cornwall). If the Saxon strategy had been to reach the Severn in order to split the Britons, the Ridgeway would definitely have been the way to come, and the real Arthur really would have walked the Marlborough Downs.

From Liddington the B4192 climbs on to the downs, crossing the M4 and following a lovely avenue of trees to Aldbourne. We, however, continue along the bottom of the downland scarp, going through **Wanborough**, where the church has an unusual 14th century hexagonal tower and spire, Hinton Parva and Bishopstone. On the downland scarp above Bishopstone are a series of staircase-like terraces: these are strip lynchets, cut to make farming the downs easier in Saxon or early medieval times. Just beyond this last village we cross into what was once Berkshire but is now part of Oxfordshire, and pass through Idstone to reach **Ashbury**, a pretty village with a neat late Norman church of white chalk and contrasting brown stone, and a rare 15th century manor house.

A short detour from Ashbury heads south-east along the B4000 to **Ashdown Park**. The house here was built by the Earl of Craven in about 1660. It is said to be in Dutch style, but Pevsner's suggestion that it is the perfect doll's house seems more appropriate. The Earl was an admirer of Charles I's sister, Elizabeth of Bohemia, the famed 'Winter Queen', and he consecrated the house to her, although she never visited it. The Earl later sent her £30,000 (a fortune at the time) to equip an army so that her son Rupert could fight to retain her husband's throne. In thanks, Elizabeth willed her collection of paintings to the Earl and some of these can be seen. Visitors are limited to certain areas of the house, chiefly the hallway, but this does allow a view of the great staircase, and the roof from which there are spectacular views of the grounds. Ashdown Woods can be visited throughout the year. To the north-west is Alfred's Castle, an early Iron Age hill-fort. The name derives from a legend that King Alfred used the fort, and it is certainly true that he defeated a Danish army in 871 somewhere locally.

Now continue along the B4507, passing the turn to Compton Beauchamp, on the left, then turn right opposite the turning to Woolstone to reach the car parks near **Uffington Castle** and the most famous of the local white horses. The castle is an early Iron Age hill-fort with a single ditch/rampart, but the white horse is a much more enigmatic creature. It is about 110m (360ft) long, and is carved on a slope of 30 degrees. It is almost impossible to see from a close approach, being best viewed from near Uffington village to the north (or from a train on the Bristol/South Wales–London main line just beyond). It is, of course, very well seen from the air, a fact which has led to the inevitable suggestions of alien carvers. Its origins are not known and, consequently, the reasons for its existence are unclear. One of the problems is that although the horse has been on the hillside for centuries it does not enter written history until the 17th century. At that time John Aubrey recorded a folk memory that the horse had been carved by followers of the Saxon leader Hengist, whose standard was a white horse. Another legend claims the horse was carved to celebrate Alfred's victory over the Danes in 871. However, modern thinking suggests that a Saxon origin is much too late, pointing to the similarities between the abstract form of the horse and those on Iron Age coins. As a result of this, many experts believe a date of the 1st century BC to be more appropriate. A pre-Saxon date is supported by the naming of Wayland's Smithy, the nearby long barrow (*see* below). Wayland was the blacksmith of the Saxon/Norse gods and rode a white horse. It is likely that the tomb was named because of the horse, implying that the horse existed when the Saxons arrived in the area. But an earlier carving presents more difficulties. If early illustrations of the horse are to be believed, then its form has changed slightly due to the turf encroaching on the cleared chalk: an 1813 illustration implies a saddle which is no longer present, and in the 19th century cleaning took place every seven years to avoid the figure being lost. If the horse is 2,000 years old, who carried out the frequent clearings, and why? The only things that can be said with certainty are that the horse is very old and that its artist was immensely skilled, creating a

Uffington White Horse

Lambourn

superb figure on a slope whose nature did not allow him (or her) a full view of the work in progress.

The beautiful sweeping combe below the horse is known as The Manger, while the curious truncated-cone hill beyond is Dragon Hill, so named because a local legend maintains it was here that St George slew the dragon. Beyond is **Uffington** village, where Thomas Hughes, the author of *Tom Brown's Schooldays* was born in 1822. **Tom Brown's School Museum** in the village has memorabilia of Hughes and of Sir John Betjeman, who also lived at Uffington, together with a collection of locally excavated items from prehistoric to Roman times.

From Uffington Castle it is worth following the Ridgeway Trail west for about 2km (1$\frac{1}{4}$ miles) to visit **Wayland's Smithy**. The long barrow stands just off the Trail, in a small copse; a lonely, slightly sinister place, the huge sarsen blocks of the façade casting strange shadows. The barrow was constructed in two phases, the earliest dating from about 2800BC. In form it is a passage with side chambers, similar to West Kennett. As noted above, the name is from Wayland, the mythical Saxon/Norse blacksmith, and legend has it that if a traveller left his horse by the barrow and a coin on a sarsen block, then the horse would be re-shod on his return.

Continue along the B4507, turning right opposite the left turn to Kingston Lisle. This steep road is Blowingstone Hill, named for a large sarsen stone (at grid reference 324871) which is pierced with curious, but natural, holes. Blowing into any one of these produces an odd trumpet-like note. Local legend has it that King Alfred used it as a war trumpet during his battles with the Danes.

The downs at the top of the hill are dotted with ancient round barrows (Bronze Age burial mounds – in one group there are at least twenty mounds, though with the eccentric logic that often applies to such sites they are called Seven Barrows) and also with numerous horse gallops: these are the Lambourn Downs, famous race-horse training grounds. The Seven Barrows are passed on our journey across the downs: bear right when the B4001 is joined to reach **Lambourn**. This large village, attractive, if not pretty, the model for Maryland in Thomas Hardy's *Jude the Obscure*, has several interesting buildings. The church is late Norman and has some excellent memorial brasses, one in the south chapel, to John of Estbury and his son dating from 1372. The memorial to Sir Thomas Essex and his wife has effigies of the couple in alabaster. Sir Thomas died in 1558. The old village stocks are now kept in the north chapel, while the churchyard holds the grave of John

Aldbourne: The village and an old fire engine in the church

Carter, the last arsonist to have been hanged in England. In the Market Place, the village cross dates from the time of Henry VI and has been restored in fine style. The almshouses close to the church date from the early 16th century but were rebuilt in 1852. They are still occupied by eight village old folk. For most of the villagers life revolves around the gallops on the downs. It is said that the Earl of Craven, builder of Ashdown House – which can be reached along the B4000 from the village – organized horse races on the downs and the tradition has been maintained.

From Lambourn, follow the minor road to **Baydon**, with its delightful chalk church, and continue to **Aldbourne**, a pretty village built around a duckpond and a green with an old cross. The church, which overlooks the green, is worth visiting to see two late 18th century fire engines (complete with instructions for use: the pair are known, inevitably, as Adam and Eve) and the carved alabaster tomb of John Stone, an early 16th century vicar. There are also some good brasses. Anciently, Aldbourne was famous for its bell foundry – chiefly making bells for animals rather than churches – and for willow and straw plaiting. The fine collection of houses implies that these were prosperous trades.

From Aldbourne there is a choice of routes. The first heads west along a minor road to reach the A345 at Ogbourne St Andrew, passing close to the site of the medieval village of **Snap**. Unlike other downland villages which were deserted when Black Death killed the inhabitants, Snap thrived until a century ago when changes in farming methods, chiefly the replacement of crops with sheep, meant fewer workers were required. In 1907 the last folk left. **Ogbourne St George**, set on the River Og (the Og Bourne), a tributary of the Kennet, is a pleasant place with a neat church beside a Jacobean manor house. Turn left along the A345, going through Ogbourne St Andrew to return to Marlborough.

The alternative route takes the B4192 from Aldbourne, soon bearing right to reach **Ramsbury**. The church here houses two coped stones from a 9th century Saxon church on the same site, and several very good memorials. Close to the church, Parliament Piece is a superb late 17th century brick house. In front of the Bell

Inn in the middle of the village stood the Ramsbury Elm, believed to have seeded when Charles I was on the throne and beneath which John Wesley preached. A local legend maintained that the spirit of Maud Toogood, a witch, inhabited the tree and there was a furore when it was decided to fell it after it succumbed to Dutch Elm Disease. The tree was also the symbol of a local building society, which planted a replacement oak tree. Perhaps Maud Toogood's spirit has taken up residence in the new tree: certainly the fears over her release into the community have proved unfounded (to date).

Continue through Ramsbury, following a minor road which, after leaving the village, zig-zags around Ramsbury Manor, a fine late 13th century house standing in equally fine parkland. The house and park are not open to the public. Just before reaching Marlborough the road goes through **Mildenhall**, the site of the Roman town of *Cunetio*, which lay to the south-east of the present village centre. The village church has excellent Regency-style box pews and a canopied pulpit and reader's desk.

ADDRESSES AND OPENING TIMES

THE MERCHANT'S HOUSE,
132 High Street, Marlborough (01672 511491)
❖
OPEN: all year, by appointment; ask at the shop which is open
Mon–Sat 10am–5pm

....

GREAT BARN/RURAL LIFE MUSEUM,
Avebury (01672 539425)
❖
OPEN: mid-March–Oct, daily 10am–5.30pm; Nov–mid-March,
Sat and Sun 11am–4.30pm

ALEXANDER KEILLER MUSEUM
(National Trust/English Heritage),
Avebury (01672 539250)

❖

OPEN: April–Oct, daily 10am-6pm or dusk if earlier;
Nov–March, daily 10am–4pm

AVEBURY MANOR AND GARDEN (National Trust),
Avebury (01672 539250)

❖

OPEN: garden, April–Oct, daily except Mon and Thurs (but
open Bank Holiday Mon) 11am–5.30pm; house, April–Oct,
Tue, Wed, Sun and Bank Holiday Mondays 2–5.30pm

SCIENCE MUSEUM ANNEX,
Wroughton Airfield (01793 814466)

❖

OPEN: on certain days only; ring for details of proposed
annual schedule

ASHDOWN HOUSE AND PARK (National Trust),
nr Ashbury and Lambourn (01488 72584)

❖

OPEN: house, April–Oct, Wed and Sat (closed at Easter and
Bank Holidays), guided tours only at 2.15pm, 3.15pm and
4.15pm; woodland, all year, Sat–Thurs, dawn to dusk

TOM BROWN'S SCHOOL MUSEUM,
Broad Street, Uffington (01367 820259)

❖

OPEN: Easter–Oct, Sat, Sun and Bank Holidays (except Aug
Bank Holiday) 2–5pm

TOUR 2: The Southern Downs and Savernake Forest

This second tour from Marlborough heads south to explore the Downs lying between the A4 and the Vale of Pewsey.

Leave Marlborough westwards, as for Tour 1, going through Fyfield before turning left to reach **West Overton**, where a 16th century manor house stands beside the church, and continuing to **East Kennett**. This is a neat village, notable for its little church and for the tree-clad long barrow set, like a giant hairy caterpillar, on the overshadowing down. The long barrow is the longest in Britain, 5m (16ft) longer than West Kennett, but has never been excavated. Such burial chambers and objects as it does contain may have damaged by the roots of the trees that now shroud it.

Return to the A4 and turn left, following the road past Silbury Hill. Cross the A361 at Beckhampton and continue towards Cherhill. As the village is approached, the Cherhill White Horse is seen to the left. The horse was cut in 1780 by men working for Dr Christopher Alsop of Calne. Alsop had the horse cut for no better reason than that he wanted to. In Calne he was known as the 'Mad Doctor' – though whether this was before or after the cutting is not clear. If before, he lived up to the title by controlling the cutting from the road, bellowing out instructions through a megaphone. In its original form the horse's eye – a significant feature over a metre (3ft) across – was made of bottles buried neck-first into the chalk so that their upturned bottoms sparkled in the sun.

The horse, which is about 38m (125ft) long and 40m (130ft) high, stands just below the ramparts of Oldbury Castle, a double ditch/rampart Iron Age hill-fort. The monument at the fort's western edge was erected in the early 1840s by Lord Lansdown as a memorial to his ancestor Sir William Petty, the 17th century economist. The downland beyond the hill-fort and monument, particularly Calstone Down, is superb walking country. Calstone Down, reached along Ranscombe Bottom from the hamlet of **Calstone Wellington** is a wonderfully folded landscape. The ham-

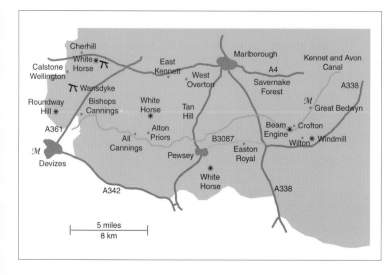

let's church is delightfully set on the slopes of the down above a small reservoir.

Calstone Wellington is reached by turning left off the A4, but before reaching the turn **Cherhill**, the village which names the white horse, is reached. In the 18th century the village was infamous as the home of a gang of highwaymen who robbed travellers on the A4's forerunner, the coach road from Bath to London. It is said that the gang attacked travellers in the nude (the robbers, that is, not the robbed) on the grounds that they were more likely to be recognized by their clothes than their faces. If true, this would seem to qualify the Cherhill gang as the most eccentric highwaymen in history. Architecturally, Cherhill village has nothing as exotic as its naked robbers, its finest building, a huge medieval tithe barn with a slated roof, having been demolished in the 1950s. But the church and the manor house beside it do make a pleasant couple.

Turning left for Calstone Wellington allows a cross-down road to be reached. Follow this to the car park where the Wansdyke crosses the road. The Wansdyke is the longest earthwork of its

Cherhill White Horse

kind in Britain, linking Dundry Hill in northern Somerset to Hampshire, a distance of 80km (50 miles), though it no longer continuous (and may never have been along its entire length). The dyke is a ditch with a bank on its southern side and is believed to date from either the late Romano-British period, perhaps built to keep out the Saxons as a final rearguard action, or by the Saxons themselves as a border between Mercian and Wessex folk. The name is certainly Saxon, from 'Woden's Dyke'. To the west of the car park the dyke is not continuous, though there is a Roman road, but to the east, from Morgan's Hill, it is, and can be followed to Marlborough and beyond.

Beyond the car park there is a golf course to the left, with Roundway Down to the right. The down was the scene, in 1643, of a major Civil War battle. After the Parliamentarian army of Sir

William Waller had been forced to yield Bath to the Royalists it regrouped here on Roundway Down. On 13 July the Royalist army under Sir Ralph Hopton arrived opposite Waller's force. Each army occupied a ridge, separated by a shallow depression. Waller's cavalry charged the Royalists, but the slight counter-gradient was too much for the horses carrying the heavily armoured troops. Their charge faltered and, sensing their chance, the Royalist cavalry charged. Waller's cavalry was routed and his infantry, confronted by enemy cavalry and, behind them, the Cornish infantry who had given them a hiding at Lansdown near Bath, turned and fled. Waller lost 600 dead, 1,000 captured and almost all his artillery: his army was effectively destroyed. It is said that each year on the anniversary of the battle, the cries of the dying can be heard echoing across the field.

Follow the road across the downland to reach the A361. Turn right towards Devizes, where the town museum includes a superb collection on Wiltshire's history and where waterway lovers will enjoy the museum devoted to the Kennet and Avon Canal. Then turn left to **Bishops Cannings**. Several places in Wiltshire claim

Calstone Down

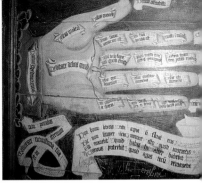

Penitential Chair
Bishops Cannings Church

to be the home of the famous 'Moonraker' myth, but Bishops Cannings' claim is better than most. The story goes that local smugglers, having hidden kegs of contraband brandy in the village pond, were using hay rakes to retrieve them one night when the excisemen arrived. When asked what they were doing the smugglers claimed they were trying to retrieve the cheese they could see in the middle of the pond. Realizing the 'cheese' was the full moon's reflection, the excisemen laughed their way out of the village and spread the word of the 'Moonrakers'. The smugglers, of course, carried on retrieving their brandy. There is no pond now in the village. The first part of Bishops Cannings' name is from the Bishop of Salisbury who 'owned' it in medieval times, this probably explaining the size, wealth and design of the village church. Its 40m (130ft) spire is a local landmark. Inside there is curious seat, its back painted with a huge hand on which are inscribed, in Latin, references to death and sin. The church organ was donated by a local man who, as a cabin boy, circumnavigated the world with Captain Cook.

To the south of Bishops Cannings the AONB extends beyond the Kennet and Avon Canal into the Vale of Pewsey, following the line of the A342. William Cobbett in his *Rural Rides*, which was published in 1830, liked the Vale, noting the 'villages, hamlets, large farms, towers, steeples, fields, meadows, orchards and very fine timber trees scattered over the valley'. It has changed little, still being a pastoral landscape. The villages that make up the Vale are invariably pretty, and an alternative to the route along the chalk scarp base is well worth considering. Heading south from Bishops Cannings the visitor reaches the A342 near Etchilhampton. Turn left along the main road passing the turn to **Conock** where there is a fine Georgian manor house. The next left turn leads to **Chirton** and **Marden** whose churches each have fine

Alton Barnes

Norman doorways. The Marden doorway includes what may be the original door, making it one of the oldest in Britain. To the north-east of Marden there is a large Neolithic henge site, an oval ditch enclosing almost 35 acres. Excavations have revealed flints, antler picks and some animal bones. Marden also has a fine early 19th century manor house and a mill on the site of one mentioned in the Domesday Book. From Marden, minor roads lead across the Vale to Pewsey.

On the scarp base, minor roads link Bishop Cannings to **All Cannings**, which also claims to be the origin of the 'Moonraker' legend – and has a pond to back the claim. The main scarp-base road continues through Stanton St Bernard to **Alton Barnes** where the church is Saxon, but with a 15th century wooden roof. The church lies just a stone's throw from the more substantial church in the neighbouring hamlet of **Alton Priors**. From the Alton villages a road crosses the downs to East Kennett. At the top of the steep section of the scarp, overlooking the village, there is a collection of interesting sites. The white horse here was cut in 1812 by Robert Pile, a local farmer, and is the biggest of all the Wiltshire horses, filling a 50m (165ft) square. Legend has it that Pile gave John Thorne, a local painter, £20 to design and cut the horse. Thorne produced a sketch, persuaded another man to start work and promptly disappeared with the £20. Pile was forced to finish the work himself: Thorne was later hanged, though it is not clear if this was simply for his theft of Pile's cash. Closer to the scarp road than the white horse is Adam's Grave, a chambered long barrow, and the remains of a Neolithic camp.

From Alton Barnes, continue along the minor road to reach **Pewsey**, the main town of the fertile Vale that separates the Marlborough Downs from Salisbury Plain. It is a pleasant market town, a statue of King Alfred gazing across the River Avon. The nearby church is memorable for the huge sarsen stones which form the foundations. To the south of the town there is another white horse, carved in 1937 by the local fire brigade to celebrate the Coronation of George VI. A little below and to the

King Alfred's Statue, Pewsey

right of the horse there is, apparently, another, carved in 1785, of which nothing can now be seen. The downland on which the horses were cut is a last section of the AONB, which follows a zig-zag course to the A338 at Collingbourne Kingston.

From Pewsey the A345 heads directly to Marlborough, passing through **Oare** where Oare House, originally built in 1740, was extended in the 1920s by Clough Williams-Ellis, the builder of Portmeirion in north Wales. Williams-Ellis also built the terrace of cottages at the south end of the village and Cold Blow at the north-western end.

Wilton Windmill

The better route is to follow the B3087 eastwards, passing the turning to **Easton Royal** where the church, built in 1591, replaced that of a monastery which was demolished after the Dissolution. When the road reaches the main road roundabout, go ahead, along the A338, then turn left in East Grafton to reach **Wilton**. To the east of the village is Wiltshire's only operating windmill, built in 1821 after the Kennet and Avon Canal had taken the water from the River Bedwyn and so prevented water mills from operating. The mill operated until 1920, when it fell into disrepair. A rescue operation was mounted in 1971 and the mill was restored in 1976. It is now a local landmark, especially when floodlit during the early evening. Guided tours of the mill are available and flour ground on-site can be bought.

From Wilton a footpath can be followed beside Wilton Water to the **Crofton Beam Engine** on the Kennet and Avon Canal. The canal was completed in 1810, linking the Avon at Bristol with, eventually, the Thames near Reading. It was an amazing feat of engineering, both from a surveying – considering its length there are remarkably few locks – and a constructional point of view. The canal, as with all those from the Golden Age of Waterways, was dug by hand, the strong-backed men who did the work giving us our slang word for a labourer: they were 'navvies', the men who dug 'navigations' as the canals were originally known. As elsewhere, the canal was made redundant by the railways. It was rescued from disuse, renovated and is now one of England's most attractive waterways, and is popular with narrow boat owners and walkers on the towpath. The canal is famous for several features along its length, most notably at Caen Hill, a short distance west of Devizes, where sixteen close-packed locks take the canal up the hill, part of a series of twenty-nine locks in a 2-mile stretch of waterway. At the Crofton Pumping Station two Cornish beam engines (dated 1812 and 1845) pumped water to the summit level of the canal. When operating, the engines were steamed from a hand-stoked boiler. The 1812 engine is the oldest operating beam engine in the world.

From Crofton follow the minor road beside the canal to **Great**

Bedwyn where the tomb of Sir John Seymour, the father of Henry VIII's third wife, Jane Seymour, can be found in the church. The church, a fine 12th century building, also has a brass to an earlier John Seymour and the stone effigy of a knight, probably dating from the early 14th century. Beside the Post Office, Lloyds the Stonemasons has been turned into an open air museum of stonecarving, with an array of tombstones and other carvings from across the years. The masons can also be seen at work. To the north of the village, **Chisbury** has an old chapel, complete with 13th century windows, that is now part of a farm, the whole farm standing within the ramparts and ditches of a late Iron Age hill-fort.

Between these two villages and Marlborough lies the **Savernake Forest**, one of the great treasures of Wiltshire. After the Conquest, the Norman kings made it a royal hunting preserve, William the Conqueror making Richard Esturmy, who had fought with him at Hastings, the Hereditary Warden of Savernake. From the Esturmys the wardenship passed to the Seymours, Sir John Seymour, whose tomb we saw at Great Bedwyn, being a Warden. It is said that Henry VIII met Jane Seymour after hunting in the forest. From the Seymours the wardenship passed to the Bruces, who became the Earls (later Marquises) of Ailesbury. It was the first Marquess who, in 1825, built Tottenham House which lies to the south-east of the forest. The house is now a school, but the church (St Katherine's, built by the second Marchioness of Ailesbury in 1861) to the north of the house can be visited. At the end of the Column Ride heading north-west from Tottenham House is a column erected by the Earl of Ailesbury in 1781. It is believed that the column previously stood in Hammersmith, London, where it had been erected about twenty years before by a gentleman wishing to commemorate his wife. It is occasionally said that Ailesbury raised the column to commemorate George III's recovery from madness, a somewhat optimistic reason if true.

In the 18th century the forest had become overgrown with thickets and Capability Brown was asked to take it in hand. Brown created the Grand Avenue, a $6^1/_2$km (4 mile) drive – $5^1/_2$km

Wilton

($3\frac{1}{2}$ miles) of it perfectly straight – from the house through the centre of the forest. At its heart he made a circus from which eight rides radiate symmetrically. In 1939, the Forestry Commission signed a 999-year lease with the Marquess, making Savernake the only large forest in Britain to be so leased.

With its great oaks – the Big Belly Oaks on the west side are said to be centuries old – beeches and chestnuts (but, sadly, no longer any elms) Savernake is a wonderful place to walk and picnic, and a haven for woodland birds and butterflies. For the lucky visitor, there may even be a glimpse of the deer whose ancestors were hunted by Henry VIII. The best way to explore the forest is from the occasional lay-by/picnic areas on the A346 or A4 which enclose it, or from the car parks off the A346 at the northern and southern tips of the forest. The forest is criss-crossed with tracks and paths, but on one day each year these are closed to visitors to prevent them becoming established rights of way.

From Chisbury or Great Bedwyn, follow minor roads to St Katherine's Church, then link to either the A346 or the A4, each of which leads back to Marlborough.

ADDRESSES AND OPENING TIMES

DEVIZES MUSEUM,
41 Long Street (01380 727369)
❖
OPEN: all year, Mon–Sat 10am–5pm

KENNET AND AVON CANAL CENTRE,
Couch Lane, Devizes (01380 721279/729489)
❖
OPEN: Easter–Christmas, daily 10am–4.30pm

WILTON WINDMILL,
Wilton (01672 870427)
❖
OPEN: Easter–Sept, guided tours only, Sun 2–5pm, Bank
Holiday Sat and Mon 2–5pm

CROFTON BEAM ENGINES,
Kennet and Avon Canal, nr Wilton (01672 870300)
❖
OPEN: Easter–Oct, daily 10.30am–5pm; steaming weekends
at various times from Easter to Aug – please ring for exact
schedules

STONEMASON MUSEUM,
Lloyd's Stonemasons, Great Bedwyn
❖
OPEN: at any reasonable time

(Opposite) The Devil's Punchbowl

THE
BERKSHIRE
DOWNS

Newbury

Although lying outside the AONB, which approaches closely on three sides, Newbury is a convenient centre for touring the eastern end of the Berkshire Downs, the downland continuation of the Marlborough Downs which falls into the deep valley taken by the River Thames. There is evidence of prehistoric and Saxon settlement of the site on which the town now stands, and the Normans built a castle here, though nothing of it survives. Newbury's position, on the main route from London to the West Country – the A4, which passes through the town, follows this old route and the M4, the new highway to the west, passes just a little way to the north – ensured its importance, though its early prosperity was largely due to one man, Jack of Newbury. Jack Winchcombe or Jack Smallwood – both names are found in the archives – is said to have arrived in Newbury with nothing and to have built up a cloth weaving business which eventually had '200 looms, 200 men, 200 pretty boys, 200 maidens and 100 women'. If Winch-

The Market Place, Newbury

combe really was Jack's name it is interesting to speculate whether he came from the Cotswold town of that name: at the time, the late 15th/early 16th centuries, the Cotswolds were the centre of the English (and European) wool trade. Jack is said to have entertained Henry VIII in Newbury; when asked to raise six men to fight the Scots, he responded by raising a hundred – fifty cavalry and fifty infantry – and marching them northwards. This patriotic tale is only spoiled by the fact that Jack's force (with himself in charge) only reached Stony Stratford in Buckinghamshire before hearing of the Scots' defeat at Flodden: they promptly turned around and went home.

Newbury was heavily involved in the English Civil War, two important battles being fought here because of the town's strategic position relative to London (Parliament's HQ) and Oxford (the King's HQ). In September 1643 the King, flushed with successes during the summer, marched on London, to be met at Newbury by the Earl of Essex's Parliamentarian army, which was returning to the capital from the siege of Gloucester. The battle that followed, fought to the south-west of the town, was inconclusive, but did cost the lives of 6,000 men. One of those, Lucius Cary, Lord Falkland, the king's Secretary of State, is commemorated in the Falkland Memorial at the battle site.

The second battle was fought to the north-west of the town, by the River Lambourn, in October 1644. This time the King was moving north from Salisbury and was intercepted by an army intent on stopping him from reaching London. Again the battle was indecisive, though it was the King who decided to retreat, taking his army back to Oxford. He left his artillery in Donnington Castle which Sir John Boys held against a concerted Parliamentarian attack. When the Parliamentarian army retreated to Newbury to regroup, the King liberated his artillery. Boys remained, however, and held the castle until the end of the war when Charles ordered him to surrender. Sir John and his force then marched out of the castle with full military honours.

A brief exploration of Newbury should start at St Nicholas' Church in Bartholomew Street. The church was built, in fine Perpendicular style, in the early 16th century by Jack of Newbury and has some excellent features including fine stained glass, a superb pulpit and the curious 'Blue Coat Boy', an effigy with a poor box, erected to collect money for support of an early 18th century school, the Blue Coat School. There is also a brass to Jack of Newbury, who died in 1519, and his wife.

From the church walk up Bartholomew Street to reach West Mills, on the left, just before Newbury bridge (Bridge Street)

West Mills and St Nicholas' Church, Newbury

ahead. The bridge was built in 1769 to replace an earlier wooden bridge over the canal. Newbury was linked to the Thames by the River Kennet Navigation which opened in 1723 and became part of the much longer Kennet and Avon Canal (from Bristol to the Thames) when that was finally completed in 1810. Go along West Mills to view Nos 15 and 16, and No. 18 which were built as almshouses in the late 17th/early 18th century. Continuing along the road, you will reach a group of early 17th century weaver's cottages, now privately owned. Return to Bartholomew Street and bear right across it to go through The Arcade (once known Whirleygog Lane) to reach Market Place. Ahead and slightly right is the Corn Exchange, in Victorian Neo-classical style. Turn left, soon passing the old Town Hall, built in 1878, which has been converted into offices. The solicitors' office opposite was once the White Hart Inn, built in the 16th century and a famous coaching inn in the 18th century. Turn right and walk down to the town's Tourist Information Centre and the West Berkshire Museum, housed in an early 18th century granary. This area is 'The Wharf', Newbury once having been an important inland port with a number of warehouses. The museum houses an interesting collection on local prehistory and the history of the town. There are sections on local geology and natural history, and an audio-visual display on the history of ballooning from 1783. The latter, a seemingly curious exhibit, includes the exploits of two local men.

Crossing the car park on the left reaches a bridge over the Kennet beyond which, to the right, is a fine park. To regain the church, reverse the route to Market Place.

One short excursion from Newbury, heading back into the AONB, is worthwhile for those visiting Donnington Castle: continue north to the Snelsmore Common Country Park, a fine area of heath and woodland with several nature trails.

Inch's Yard, Newbury

TOUR 3: The Southern Downs
This first tour from Newbury heads south, following the Downs as they decline in height and cross the county boundary into Hampshire.

From Newbury take the A4 westwards, re-entering the AONB near Stockcross and continuing to **Hungerford**, a relatively new town, having no recorded or excavated history before the 12th century. By the 17th century the town was reasonably prosperous: Samuel Pepys ate at the Bear Inn (which dates from the 15th century) in 1668, and twenty years later the same inn was the venue for a meeting between William of Orange and representatives of James II, a meeting which led to the fall of the Stuarts. Later, the town was an important coach stop on the road from London to Bath, and then a port on the Kennet and Avon Canal. It was after the opening of the latter, in 1810, that the town church was built (though the medieval one it replaced fell down rather than being demolished), a large but none-too-interesting building, though the bow window at the east end is a remarkable ecclesiastical feature. To see the best of the town go to the High Street, where a fire which destroyed all the medieval buildings allowed a complete rebuild in fine, and unified, 18th century style.

Hungerford is one of the few English towns which retains a manorial court, complete with an official ale taster, and also has a curious old custom. This, Tutti Day, is enacted on the second Tuesday after Easter and involves two 'tutti' men carrying long poles decorated with ribbons and flowers (tutti is the local word for a bunch of flowers) who call on specific houses (as laid down in an ancient document) to collect a 'head penny', an old form of poll tax collected by the manorial lord. The strange part of the custom was that the tutti men were required to share a drink with the householder, give him an orange and kiss his wife, a somewhat dubious collection of duties. As there are over a hundred houses on the tutti men's list the day can be a long, and ultimately unsteady, one.

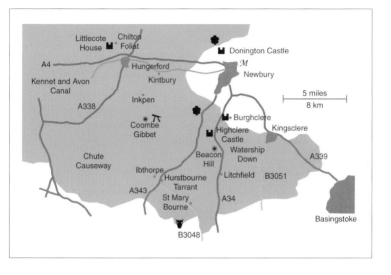

To the north-west of Hungerford – follow the B4192 – is
Chilton Foliat, just over the border in Wiltshire. This neat little
village with its Georgian houses was given by Henry VIII to each
of his wives in turn. Just across the Kennet from the village is **Littlecote House**, one of the finest houses in Wiltshire, indeed, one
of the finest Tudor mansions in Britain. The site is an ancient one,
a Roman villa with a fine mosaic floor having been excavated in
the grounds. The present house was built on the site of an earlier
manor house by the Dornell family. One head of the family is said
to have claimed *droit de seigneur* on a lady-in-waiting and to have
thrown the baby she bore on to a fire, leaving the house haunted
by the lady vainly searching for her child and the shrieks of the
infant. For all that, a visit is worthwhile: the house's Great Hall
and Long Gallery (over 30m, almost 110ft, long) are superb.
Henry VIII is said to have wooed Jane Seymour here and their initials are entwined in the stained glass of the Great Hall. Visitors
to the house can view the Roman villa; there is also a licensed coffee house.

67

The downland to the south of the Kennet Valley is lovely country, but is criss-crossed by a maze of minor roads linking tiny villages. Many of these are extremely picturesque, but a route linking them all could only be contemplated by the most ardent completist. Here we trace a diagonal route across the area, visiting the best of the sites, but taking the occasional detour.

From Hungerford, take the minor road east towards Kintbury, then bear right on the road through Lower Green, climbing **Inkpen Hill** to the car park near its summit. This is the last section of chalk downland, and a fine walk (along a bridleway) heads eastward over Walbury Hill and along the scarp top, or west along the scarp edge of Inkpen Hill itself. Walbury Hill is topped by an Iron Age hill-fort and, at 297m (974ft), is the highest chalk hill in England – and the highest point in Berkshire – but Inkpen (a little lower at 291m, 954ft) has a more interesting, if more gruesome, summit structure. There stands a gaunt gibbet (Coombe Gibbet), unusual in being in good repair – the lease of the tenant farmer who works the land requires him to keep it in good repair (does the lease actually say 'good working order' ?!) – and in having a T-bar top rather than the more conventional single arm.

Inkpen Hill

The gibbet was erected in 1676 to dispatch George Broomham and Dorothy Newman, who had murdered Broomham's wife and son. The gibbet was used only on that one occasion, despite having been replaced twice, once after being struck by lightning and then when the first replacement rotted away. The story of the murders was the basis of the 1948 film *The Black Legend*.

To the north of the hill, **Inkpen** village is a straggling – but pretty – place, its name deriving not from any literary association but from 'Inga's Pen', the animal pen of Inga, a Saxon landowner. Interestingly, until the early 20th century the village was

Coombe Gibbet

famous for its potters, and a spectacular beaker of the Beaker Folk, the tallest ever found, was unearthed nearby: the local clay has supplied potters for over 4,000 years. Inkpen Common, to the east of the village, is a Nature Reserve set up to protect 26 acres of acidic gravel lying on chalk which has a unique flora. The wild crocus is especially profuse, but there are also patches of dwarf gorse and rare flowers such as lousewort. Bog asphodel thrives in patches of bog, and there is also fine woodland of birch and oak. The common is also good for butterflies and birds. North again, at **Kintbury** it is claimed that a Lt Dexter was buried in the churchyard complete with his sword and that those who visit the yard at night can hear the sword rattling in his coffin.

Continue along the road over Inkpen Hill, crossing the Hampshire border to reach Linkenholt. A short detour westwards from here is of interest to Roman scholars as the Roman road from Winchester to Mildenhall (*Cunetio*) makes a spectacular curve to avoid the deep Hippenscombe Valley and is a clear causeway (now carrying a minor road) as it bears west then north to regain a point from which it could continue in a straight line.

Follow minor roads through Upton to **Ibthorpe**, often claimed to be the prettiest village in Hampshire, and **Hurstbourne Tarrant** where the church has early 14th century murals. William Cobbett, in his *Rural Rides*, claimed that he had never seen more reclusive villages than those he visited in this secluded part of north Hampshire: it is still the same, the folded country seemingly intent on keeping intruders at bay. Continue to **St Mary Bourne**, looking for the Victorian flint and brick almshouses to the north-west of the church. To the south of the village, and on the edge of the AONB, is the **Finkley Down Farm Park** where children can make friends with farm animals and pets, ride mini-tractors and enjoy the adventure playground. There is also a large picnic area.

Highclere Castle from Beacon Hill

Bear left at St Mary Bourne to reach the A34 and turn left towards Newbury, passing through pleasant, pastoral country. **Litchfield**, alive with flowers, lies just off the main road, which then cuts through a series of Bronze Age round barrows known as Seven Barrows. Soon the downland edge is reached: to the left is **Beacon Hill**. The hill is an excellent viewpoint, particularly of the Highclere Estate to the north, but is most famous for the grave of the 5th Earl of Carnarvon. Carnarvon financed the excavations of Howard Carter which led to the discovery in 1922 of the untouched tomb of Tutankhamun with its fabulous riches. The tomb had an inscription cursing anyone daring to disturb it and the Earl's death during the excavations led to public interest and Hollywood's enthusiasm for the 'curse of the Pharaohs'. There are occasional attempts to ascribe some form of curse to Beacon Hill, but quite what form this would take and to whom is vague. There is a car park at the base of the hill, reached by turning off the A34.

Highclere Castle, beyond the hill, is the seat of the Earls of Carnarvon. Originally owned by the Bishops of Winchester, when the estate came to the Carnarvon family they had the original house rebuilt using, as architect, Sir Charles Barry who was also responsible for the Houses of Parliament, the similarity between the two being quite striking. The interior of the house is as ornate as the exterior and there is a collection of artwork that is equally rich, including paintings by Reynolds, Gainsborough and Van Dyck. There is also a fine collection of 18th and 19th century furniture and a fascinating exhibition on the discovery of the tomb of Tutankhamun.

Outside the castle, the grounds in which it stands are equally attractive. The parkland was designed by Capability Brown and includes huge Lebanon cedars over 200 years old, several lakes and superb viewpoints of the castle. There is also a classical temple built in the 18th century, but remodelled by Sir Charles Barry. Roe and muntjac deer are often seen in the park. There are also two fine gardens, a walled one which dates from the previous house on the site and the 'Secret Garden' with lawns and herbaceous borders. The castle has a licensed tea room.

But we are ahead of ourselves. Before reaching Highclere on the minor road which leaves the A34 to reach the Beacon Hill car park, turn right to reach Old Burghclere. Continue along the minor road, passing Sydmonton, then turn right at a crossroads and climb steeply on to the Down. This is **Watership Down**, once known only to walkers. Since the publication of Richard Adams' rabbit saga (called *Watership Down*) it is internationally known and a place of pilgrimage for lovers of the book. A footpath crosses the Down, heading east to reach a car park on White Hill (on the B3051 – the car park is a much better approach to the Down). It is also possible to head west, following the scarp edge to Ladle Hill where there is an Iron Age hill-fort and a Bronze Age round barrow.

The minor road past Sydmonton can be followed to **Kingsclere** where the church has a fine Purbeck marble font and some early 16th century memorial brasses; there are also some fine 18th century houses in Swan Street. From Kingsclere the B3051 heads southwards, climbing White Hill to explore the final part of the AONB. From Kingsclere, Newbury can be regained by following the A339, the final section of that road going through superb

Sandham Memorial Chapel

Stanley Spencer's Resurrection, *Sandham Memorial Chapel*

woodland and passing the Greenham Common women's peace camp.

Back on the road to Highclere Castle, go past the entrance to reach a road junction with a turn to Woolton Hill on the left. Continue towards **Burghclere**, soon reaching the Sandham Memorial Chapel. The red brick chapel was built in the 1920s by Mr and Mrs J. L. Behrend as a memorial to a relative who was killed during the First World War. It is remarkable for its decoration, a series of nineteen frescoes by Stanley Spencer. Spencer was a Red Cross orderly and, later, a soldier in the same war and the paintings are a moving account of the life of the ordinary soldier. At the chapel's eastern end is a huge painting of the Resurrection, its foreground a heap of wooden crosses handed in by individual soldiers. Resurrections usually include Christ in Judgement, but here

He is a figure of comfort in a brilliant work. Please note that the chapel, which is now in the care of the National Trust, is unlit and so the paintings are best viewed on a very bright day.

Now return to the road junction and turn right towards **Woolton Hill**, a village with a good flint church, which lies the other side of the A343. Just to the south of the village is the **Hollington Herb Garden**, a one-acre walled garden divided into 'sub-gardens' by box hedges and planted with roses, climbers and the herbs of the name. There is also a nursery where plants grown at the garden can be bought.

From Woolton Hill, return to the A343 and turn left to return to Newbury, passing close to the Falkland Memorial.

ADDRESSES AND OPENING TIMES

DONNINGTON CASTLE (English Heritage),
Newbury
❖
OPEN: at any reasonable time,
for viewing of the exterior only

WEST BERKSHIRE MUSEUM
(also called the Newbury District Museum),
The Wharf, Newbury (01635 30511)

OPEN: April–Sept, Mon, Tues and Thur–Sat 10am–5pm,
Sun 1-5pm; Oct–March, Mon, Tue and Thur–Sat 10am–4pm;
also open Wed (same times) during school holidays

SNELSMORE COMMON COUNTRY PARK,
North of Donnington Castle, Newbury (01635 519620)
❖
OPEN: any reasonable time

LITTLECOTE HOUSE,
nr Hungerford (01488 682509)
❖
OPEN: June–Oct, Sun and Wed 11am–4pm

FINKLEY DOWN FARM PARK,
nr Walworth Industrial Estate, Andover (01264 352195)
❖
OPEN: mid-March–Oct, daily 10am–6pm

HIGHCLERE CASTLE,
(01635 253210)
❖
OPEN: early May–late Sept, Tue–Fri, Sun and Bank Holiday
Mon 11am–5pm, Sat 11am–3.30pm; last admission one
hour before closing time

SANDHAM MEMORIAL CHAPEL,
Burghclere (01635 278394)
❖
OPEN: April–Oct, Wed–Sun and Bank Holiday Mon (but then
closed on following Wed) 11.30am–5pm; March and Nov,
Sat and Sun 11.30am–4pm; Dec–Feb, by appointment only

HOLLINGTON HERB GARDEN,
Woolton Hill (01635 253908)
❖
OPEN: March–Sept, daily 11am–4.30pm

TOUR 4: The Northern Downs

This tour explores the Berkshire Downs, the continuation of Wiltshire's chalk downland, which ends at the Thames Valley. It also crosses the Oxfordshire border to explore the northern edge of the chalk.

From Newbury, take the A4 east towards Thatcham. After $1^1/_2$km (1 mile), turn right along Lower Way then, after a further $^3/_4$km ($^1/_2$ mile) turn right into Muddy Lane to reach the **Thatcham Discovery Centre**. Although outside the AONB, few visitors will want to miss this fascinating site. In association with the Royal Society for the Protection of Birds and English Nature, the centre preserves the largest remaining inland reedbed in Britain, a home to reed and sedge warblers and the day-flying Scarlet Tiger Moth. The centre also has a regular programme of exhibitions and events, many centred on the local natural history.

Return to the main road and turn right. Beyond two roundabouts and Colthrop, to the right, turn left towards Upper Bucklebury, bearing right to cross **Bucklebury Common**, a fine area of mixed woodland crossed by numerous paths. An attempt to enclose the Common was defeated in 1835 when John Morton, a local farmer and lay preacher, went to Westminster and spoke in opposition to the proposal. From the eastern edge of the Common a superb avenue of oaks heads east-north-east. It is said that the first avenue was planted to commemorate a visit by Elizabeth I, further trees being added to celebrate the victories at Blenheim and Waterloo. More recently, trees have been planted to celebrate a visit by Elizabeth II and the 80th birthday of Queen Elizabeth, the Queen Mother. The road through the avenue leads to **Englefield** where the house dates from Elizabethan times, though it was rebuilt after a fire in 1886. Sir Francis Walsingham was an inhabitant of the earlier building. The house has a deer park with a herd of fallow deer, but at present neither is open to the public.

Our route does not visit Englefield, heading north instead to **Stanford Dingley**, an extremely attractive village. The delightful

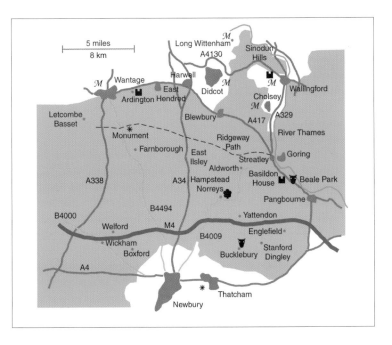

tree-shrouded flint church is dedicated, unusually, to St Denys. The saint was martyred in 3rd century France, legend having it that his body stood up, picked up his head and walked to his chosen burial spot, the story explaining the carving on the lectern. To reach the village we have crossed the River Pang: turn left beyond the church, following a road parallel to the river, then recrossing it to reach **Bucklebury**, whose medieval manorial lord was John Winchcombe, the son of Jack of Newbury. A later Winchcombe, Frances, married a rising politician, Henry St John, Lord Bolingbroke, and turned their home into a gathering place for society folk and the literati. Alexander Pope came here, Dean Swift is said to have preached in the village church – a pleasant building with a fine Norman doorway and good stained glass – and Queen Anne probably visited too, Bolingbroke being her Secretary of State. But Bolingbroke's pay and Frances' fortune could not maintain the pace and when the money ran out Bolingbroke's career abruptly ended: he fled to France where he met another rich lady, leaving his wife with the debts and debtors. She is said to have died of stress and a broken heart. Just outside the village is **Buckleberry Farm Park** where tractors carry visitors to see the farm's herd of red deer. There is also a farm trail, an adventure playground and a picnic area. At the right time of year visitors will see lambs and young deer.

From Bucklebury head west, following the River Pang at first, then bearing away from it to reach **Hermitage**, set among fine woodland. A walk to Grimsbury Castle, an Iron Age hill-fort, is worthwhile as walkers may see muntjac deer (though they are extremely elusive) and will certainly see Grimsbury Tower, an 18th century embattled octagonal brick tower, now a private house.

Hermitage lies on the B4009: turn right along this, soon reaching **Hampstead Norreys**, another very attractive village, the old

Wyld Court Rainforest Conservation Centre

well and stone water troughs now filled with flowers. The second part of the name recalls a 15th century manorial lord, Sir John Norreys. A later member of the family, Henry Norreys, was executed by Henry VIII for alleged adultery with Anne Boleyn, though strangely his son became a leading soldier under Elizabeth I, Anne Boleyn's daughter. The village church is 12th century, but incorporates details from an earlier, Saxon building. The church has a fine beamed roof and a marvellous sculpture of a knight on horseback whose origins and purpose are now lost.

From Hampstead Norreys the B4009 crosses the River Pang. The road now continues through beautiful country to reach Streatley, soon passing the **Rainforest Conservation Centre** at Wyld Court. Here three different rainforest climates – Lowland Tropical, Cloud Forest and Amazonica – have been created under glass, with both flora and fauna species. The centre is owned by the World Land Trust, which is committed to saving the world's diminishing areas of rainforest. The Trust buys rainforest throughout the world and runs Wyld Court as both a conservation and education centre. A worthy cause and a marvellous site.

Our tour leaves the B4009 before Wyld Court, turning right to reach **Yattendon** where Monica, the daughter of the late 19th century manorial lord Alfred Waterhouse, married the poet, later Poet Laureate, Robert Bridges. The couple lived in the Manor House where Bridges and Professor Ellis Wooldridge produced the Yattendon Hymnal, Bridges writing the words of hymns set to old Berkshire tunes. Bridges was also responsible for the Yattendon Psalter. At his request, he was not buried or commemorated by an elaborate tomb, his ashes being scattered in the churchyard.

From Yattendon, follow minor roads running parallel to the M4, passing Pangbourne Tower, built in the 1890s in the William and Mary style and now a Nautical College, to reach **Pangbourne**, at the edge of the AONB, a town set where the River Pang meets the Thames. Church Cottage, which stands beside the 17th century church, was the retirement home of Kenneth Grahame, the author of *The Wind in the Willows*. Grahame, one-time secretary to the Bank of England, married late in life and compiled the book from stories he told to his only son. It is likely that Grahame was inspired by the local riverside scenery, scenery which also inspired *Three Men in a Boat*, in which Jerome K. Jerome has his heroes stay at Pangbourne's Swan Hotel. Less famous is Tom Carter, a Pangbourne man who became Lord Nelson's favourite bo'sun. He is buried in the churchyard.

From the town, follow the A329 north-westwards along the Thames Valley, soon reaching **Beale Park** on the right. Here, on 300 acres of ancient water meadows, rare breeds of sheep, goat, cattle and deer – and the only breed of llama – can be seen. About 45 acres of woodland have been planted and at the river's edge a reedbed is being restored to encourage native wildlife. There is a pets' corner and adventure playground for children, and a model boat collection which will appeal to both children and adults. There is also a collection of sculptures in classical style, amassed by Gilbert Beale who also built the classically-styled pavilion which houses the model boats. The site also includes several aviaries, a narrow-gauge railway, a willow maze, a cafeteria and a picnic site.

A short distance beyond Beale Park, to the left, is **Basildon Park**, a superb Palladian mansion in Bath stone built in the 1770s for Sir Francis Sykes, who had made a fortune trading in India. The house is huge, but so well balanced that it is not in the least ostentatious. The interior is notable for its original plasterwork and the open well staircase which ascends three storeys to an arched gallery. There is also a curious Octagon room, probably added in Victorian times by J.B. Papworth. The house was elegantly furnished by Lord and Lady Iliffe in the early 20th century when they rescued it from neglect. Outside, the early 19th century pleasure gardens are being restored and there are waymarked trails through the parkland, some leading to viewpoints with panoramic views of the downs.

Continue along the main road to reach **Streatley**, a beautifully positioned village just across the Thames from **Goring**, the bigger village which gives its name to the 'gap' or gorge through which the Thames flows. There is an unspoken, but nonetheless clear,

Beale Park

Basildon Park

rivalry between the two villages, Streatley claiming to be the superior of the two, Goring having all the amenities, a fact which might commend it to most folk but which Streatley sees as being too commercial and therefore a little downmarket. Legend has it that in cricket matches between the two villages there have been more batsmen injured by misdirected balls than might be expected and the cricket pavilion has been burnt down several times. Interestingly, as the boundary of Goring (and, as a consequence, the border between Berkshire – in which Streatley stands – and Oxfordshire) lies on the Streatley side of the river, technically Goring owns the Thames.

From Streatley the B4009 climbs steeply up on to the Downs, on its way to Hampstead Norreys, passing through fine woodland – there is a car park at the top from where short walks lead to superb views of Goring Gap – to reach **Aldworth** where the church houses what is claimed to be the best collection of early 14th century effigies in Britain. There are eight, all of members of the De la Beche family, of which they are thought to represent three generations. The effigies were damaged by the Puritans, but are still powerful pieces of work, the best being that on the north side of the church of a reclining knight, his head once on his hand as he leaned on his elbow. The locals called the effigies the Aldworth Giants and had individual names – John Long, John Strong – for each. They claim that there was once one more, known as John Ever-afraid, who had made a pact with the Devil who would claim his soul if he was buried in a church or churchyard. To solve the puzzle of how to prevent eternal damnation the body, and the effigy, were buried beneath a wall of the church, that is neither in the church nor the churchyard.

Continue north along the A329 from Streatley, then bear right (still on the A329) to reach **Wallingford**. The Thames could be forded here – hence the latter part of the name – and it is likely that the site was first settled by the Romans. It was certainly settled by the Saxons, who fortified the town. Sections of the fortifi-

The Thames at Goring

cations can still be seen: to the north-east of the town, behind the museum, Bull Croft, a recreation area, is bounded on two sides by a Saxon ditch, and the banks which bound Kine Croft – opposite the museum – are also Saxon. In 1006 the Danes under Sweyn attacked the town, completely destroying it, though its strategic importance meant that it was soon rebuilt. The Normans built a motte and bailey, and over the years the castle expanded to include three rings of walls and a central keep, the whole attached to a town wall. Wallingford's impor-

An Aldworth Giant

tance in Norman England can be seen from the fact that a priory was built here and it was in the castle that the Treaty of Wallingford was signed, ending the civil war between Stephen and Matilda and ensuring the succession of Henry II. Perhaps in gratitude, when Stephen died and Henry became king he granted the town a charter which ensured its continued prosperity. Later, in 1420 when Henry V gave Wallingford Castle to Queen Katherine, Thomas, the son of Geoffrey Chaucer, was made constable.

There was a slump in the town's prosperity in the late medieval period, with disease and fire taking its toll of townsfolk and buildings. The Dissolution, which closed the priory (of which nothing survives) also contributed to the decline, monasteries virtually guaranteeing prosperity for the towns beside them. Then in the Civil War, the Royalists held the castle against a Parliamentarian siege. Only when the King, realizing his cause was lost, ordered its surrender did the garrison give up. Six years later Cromwell ordered the castle's demolition, a job which was carried out with such enthusiasm that almost nothing remains.

The Market Place, Wallingford

The loss of the castle completed the reduction in Wallingford's fortunes, but since that time it has quietly regained its confidence and is today a delightful place, well worth an exploratory walk. The walk should start at the Tourist Information Centre which is housed in the Town Hall in Market Place.

The Town Hall was built in 1670, replacing an earlier Guild Hall – which stood the other side of St Mary-le-More Church. With its Venetian windows, on the Market Place side, and colonnaded ground floor it has great character. When built, the first floor was the town courtroom: from it the balcony could be reached for public pronouncements. In 1956 Queen Elizabeth II stood on the balcony to the delight of Wallingford folk massed in Market Place. The square itself is an elegant place, defined by buildings largely from the early 19th century (apart from the Town Hall of course).

Go to the left of the Town Hall, passing the mid-19th century flint-built church of St Mary-le-More and continuing through St Leonard's Square to reach St Leonard's Lane, on the left. This leads to St Leonard's Church, the oldest of the three churches in the town: at the height of its prosperity Wallingford boasted fifteen churches. St Leonard's is Norman, but was damaged by fire during the Civil War and then badly restored by the Victorians.

Bear left along Thames Street to reach St Peter's Church, on the right. The original church was destroyed during the siege of Wallingford Castle in 1646 and was rebuilt in the 1760s. The spire, open-work in four stages and set on an octagonal openwork bell tower, was added in 1777 and is quite charming, one of the highlights of the town. At the High Street a right turn leads to the Thames bridge which, at over 250m (800ft), is one of the longest across the river. It is likely that there was a bridge here in Norman, perhaps even Saxon, times but the present 19-arch structure dates from the 15th or early 16th century. The bridge has always been central to Wallingford's prosperity, tolls being collected on land traffic over it and river traffic under it, and bridge maintenance being the responsibility of two Bridgemen was sat on the town's Corporation. Today the Town Council still has two Bridgemen, though they are symbolic. The Thames is the scene of the Wallingford Regatta, held each year at the end of May and one of the most prestigious events on the British rowing calendar. The river bank is also excellent for a quiet stroll.

Turn left at St Peter's, or return from the bridge, following High Street. Nos 17–19 are 16th century buildings and extremely picturesque. Calleva House is Georgian, its name deriving from the mistaken view that Wallingford was the site of Roman town of *Calleva* (which has now been shown to be at Silchester). The George Inn is 16th century and a local legend maintains that Dick Turpin, the famous highwayman, once stayed here. Turn right along Castle Street, then right again along Bear Lane to reach a doorway, on the left, leading to the Castle Gardens and the remains of the castle. The doorway marks the position of the outer wall of the castle, the gardens occupying the outer bailey. Climb the steps ahead to reach the line of the second wall. A bridge over Castle Lane now gives access to the motte from where there is a fine view of the spire of St Peter's Church. Of the castle, little remains – a section of wall towards the river and, on the town side, the ruined tower of what is believed to have been the castle's chapel.

Return to High Street and turn right, continuing along it. Soon, to the right, is the entrance to Bull Croft. Further on, to the left, is Goldsmith's Lane. In Saxon times Wallingford had a mint – a sign of its importance – which is believed to have stood in this street. Just beyond, on the right, is Flint House. This stands on the site of Wallingford Priory. When Cardinal Wolsey dissolved the priory in 1524 it was to obtain the cash he needed to fund his building of Cardinal (now Christ Church) College, Oxford. The stone of the priory was used by John Norreys to build the façade of a timber-framed house – Flint House. Norreys' house was single storey, the second storey being added later. Today the house is home to Wallingford Museum where the history of the town is explored in an excellent display which employs sound as well as standard exhibition techniques.

Opposite the museum is Kine Croft, thought to have been a cattle grazing area in Saxon times. To complete a fine explanatory walk, follow the Saxon ditch which borders it to reach Mill Lane, turning left, then right and left again to return to Market Place.

Finally, railway enthusiasts will want to visit Wallingford railway station. After the closure of the British Rail branch line from Cholsey in 1981, the line was acquired by enthusiasts who re-opened it in 1994. Today the Cholsey and Wallingford Railway runs steam and diesel trains along the line on certain days. **Cholsey** is outside the AONB, but is a place of pilgrimage for Agatha Christie fans as she is buried in St Mary's Churchyard. Wallingford Station has a museum of railway memorabilia, a model of the original station and an N-gauge model railway.

The AONB completes a circle at Wallingford, following a crooked finger of highland around the lowland to the east of the town. We follow that finger, heading north-west along the A4130,

Castle Gardens, Wallingford

then turning right beyond Brighwell-cum-Sotwell to round the Sinodun Hills, topped by an Iron Age hill-fort (on Castle Hill) and offering a fine view (from Round Hill) of the Thames and the Roman town of Dorchester beyond. The hills form part of the **Little Wittenham Nature Reserve** which also includes Little Wittenham Wood and a section of Thames river bank. The Reserve has an interesting flora, including the Loddon lily, good butterflies and birds, and muntjac deer in the woodland. Go through Little Wittenham village and on to **Long Wittenham** which has a fine Norman Church and a good example of a cruck-built house – Cruckfield Cottage – near the village cross. The village is also home to the **Pendon Museum** which reproduces the 1930s Vale of White Horse in miniature, with cottages, farms, lanes and a GWR branch line with steam engines. The models have been built up over a period of forty years and are exquisite.

From Long Wittenham, railway enthusiasts will want to visit the **Didcot Railway Centre** for its collection of GWR memorabilia including several steam locomotives, but to stay in the AONB, follow minor roads to North and South Moreton and on to **Blewbury** where the church has early and late Norman features. There is also a single almshouse, built in 1738 to accommodate the oldest man in the village. The village's second oldest man must have had difficulty in forcing out congratulations and hopes for a long life on the oldest's birthday. Kenneth Grahame lived in the village from 1910 to 1924.

On the downs above Blewbury the Ridgeway National Trail descends towards the Thames, walkers having views northward over horse gallops. The last good section of downland walking on the route lies further west and we shall visit it from Wantage. To reach the town, follow the A417, crossing the A34 near **Harwell** village, where there are almshouses dating from the early 18th century. The local area is famous for its fruit orchards – buy from the stalls and farm shops for good, fresh stock – and for the Atomic Energy Research Establishment which, surprisingly, lies within the AONB. Today much of the research here is into the medical and industrial uses of radiation rather than power production.

Continue past **East Hendred**, where there is a vineyard producing white wine – the small shop there is open for tasting and buying – and the turning to West Hendred, then turn left into **Ardington** to see Ardington House, a red and grey brick building dating from 1721. In the hall there is a good stairway and the panelled dining room has a fine painted ceiling. Continue into **Wantage**, famous as the birthplace (in 849) of Alfred the Great, whose statue gazes across the Market Place. Alfred was King of Wessex and scored a number of victories over the encroaching Danes before being forced to retreat to the safety of the Somerset Levels. There he regrouped and emerged to secure a Saxon England. Close to the Market Place is St Peter and St Paul's Church which is worth visiting for its memorials which include several good brasses, one from the early 14th century, and alabaster effigies. The town's Vale and Downland Museum, housed in a 16th century cloth merchant's house and a reconstructed barn, explores the geology and history of the Vale of White Horse, the local downland and the town.

To explore the local downland it is necessary to make a short detour from Wantage before returning to Newbury. Take the B4507 westwards, then turn left through Letcombe Regis to **Letcombe Bassett** where Thomas Hardy stayed while writing *Jude the Obscure*, in which the village appears as 'Cresscombe'. From the village, Gramp's Hill rises on the Downs. Where the Ridgeway National Trail crosses the road – parking is tricky, but feasible – a short walk west (right) allows a view of the Devil's Punchbowl, a sweeping incut of the Downs. In the other direction, Segsbury Castle, an Iron Age hill-fort, is soon reached.

To return to Newbury from Wantage, take the B4494, parking at the Down crest where the Ridgeway crosses the road (there is a car park here). Now walk east, soon reaching a monument to Robert Lloyd-Lindsay, Lord Wantage (1832–1901) a holder of the Victoria Cross. To the left here is a section of Grim's Ditch, a prehistoric rampart/ditch which follows the scarp edge for some distance, both east and west. The name is Saxon, from Grim, a god synonymous with Odin: the Saxons, as was usual with features beyond their understanding, believed the ditch was the work of the gods. Continue eastwards, passing a reservoir on the left, beside which is a memorial stone to Sir John Betjeman's wife. Now follow the Trail to the top of Cuckhamsley Hill to find the tree-shrouded Scutchamer Knob, probably a long barrow. The name is curious: it could be Saxon, from their chieftain Cwichelm who may also have named the hill (and could, perhaps, be buried in the mound) or from scutcher, said to be the local name for flax beaters, who held an annual festival here.

Back on the tour, continue south along the B4494, turning left to Farnborough where the church has a window dedicated to Sir John Betjeman by the artist John Piper. The quick way back to Newbury now continues eastwards, going through West Ilsley to reach East Ilsley. The villages are thought to be named from the Saxon word for a battlefield – another of Alfred's battles with the Danes? **East Ilsley** is well known for its racing stables, explaining the gallops beside the Ridgeway to the east. Anciently it was

The Wantage Memorial

more famous for sheep rearing, an old rhyme maintaining it was:

> Far famed for sheep and wool, though not for spinners
> For sportsmen, doctors, publicans and sinners

Clearly a God-fearing village. From East Ilsley follow the A34 south to Newbury.

The longer return from Farnborough follows the B4494, perhaps with detours to some of the picturesque local villages, Brightwalton or Boxford. **Boxford**, lying in the Lambourn Valley, has a pleasant church with a 17th century tower. Further up the valley is **Welford** where Henry VIII had a hunting lodge on the site now occupied by Welford Park. In nearby **Wickham** the church has a Saxon tower and a surprising interior. On the reredos there are eight carved angels, but the real joy are the papier-mâché elephants which appear to hold up the aisle roof. The original three were bought by the vicar at the Paris Exhibition of 1862, but proved too large for the rectory.

The minor road in the Lambourn Valley or the B4494 can now be used to return to Newbury.

ADDRESSES AND OPENING TIMES

THATCHAM DISCOVERY CENTRE,
Muddy Lane, Lower Way, Thatcham (01635 874381)
❖
OPEN: April–Sept, Tues–Fri 12noon–3pm (11am–5pm in school holidays), Sat and Sun 11am–5pm; Bank Holiday Mon 11am–5pm; Oct–March, Tues–Fri 12noon–3pm, Sat and Sun 12noon–4pm

BUCKLEBURY FARM PARK,
Bucklebury (0118 971 4002)
❖
OPEN: Good Friday–mid-Sept, Fri–Sun 10am–6pm and daily in school holidays, same times

WYLD COURT RAINFOREST CONSERVATION CENTRE,
Hampstead Norreys (01635 200221 [recorded] or 202444)
❖
OPEN: March–Oct, daily 10am–5.30pm; Nov–Feb, daily
10am–4.30pm; closed Christmas Day and Boxing Day

BEALE PARK,
Lower Basildon (0118 984 5172)
❖
OPEN: March–23 Dec, daily 10am–6pm
(5pm or dusk in March and Oct–Dec)

BASILDON PARK,
Lower Basildon (0118 984 3040)
❖
OPEN: house, April–Oct, Wed–Sun 1–5.30pm (also open on
Bank Holiday Mon, but closed on Good Friday); park and
garden, April–Oct, Wed–Sun 11.30am–5.30pm (also open
Bank Holiday Mon, but closed on Good Friday), March, Sat
and Sun 12noon–5pm

CASTLE GARDENS AND RUINS,
Bear Lane, Wallingford (01491 826972)
❖
OPEN: April–Oct, daily 10am–6pm

WALLINGFORD MUSEUM,
Flint House, High Street, Wallingford (01491 835065)
❖
OPEN: March–Nov, Tues–Fri 2–5pm, Sat 10.30am–5pm;
also open on Sun 2–5pm from June–Aug
and Bank Holidays 2–5pm

CHOLSEY AND WALLINGFORD RAILWAY
(01491 835067)
❖
Six trains daily on certain days from Easter–Oct – ring for
timetable; the Wallingford Station Museum is open
11am–5pm on days when trains are running

PENDON MUSEUM,
Long Wittenham, (01865 407365)
❖
OPEN: Jan–Nov, Sat and Sun 2–5pm; also open on Wed
from June–Aug, same time, and from 11am–5pm over
Easter period and on Bank Holiday weekends

DIDCOT RAILWAY CENTRE,
Didcot Parkway Railway Station (01235 817200)
❖
OPEN: Easter–Sept, daily 10am–5pm; Oct and March, Sat
and Sun 10am–5pm; Nov–Feb, Sat and Sun 11am–4pm;
also open daily during certain school holidays

ARDINGTON HOUSE,
Ardington (01235 833244)
❖
OPEN: May–Sept, Mon 2.30–4.30pm

VALE AND DOWNLAND MUSEUM,
Church Street, Wantage (01235 771447)
❖
OPEN: All year, Tue–Sat 10.30am–4.30pm, Sun 2.30–5pm

(Opposite) All Souls College from St Mary's Church Tower, Oxford

OXFORD

Oxford

Oxford, the city of dreaming spires. Matthew Arnold's famous quote – what he actually said was 'that sweet city with her dreaming spires' – is known by almost every visitor to Oxford. Yet for all its perceptiveness, the visitor needs to be away from the city to fully appreciate Arnold's words. Go to Jarn Mound at Boar's Hill, about 5km (3 miles) to the south-west, stand and be entranced.

Although there have been finds from the Stone, Bronze and Iron Ages close to the city centre, it is believed that these were isolated settlements and not evidence of even a minor town. It is believed that a Roman road crossed the Thames close to where Folly Bridge now stands, but even that seems to have been servicing a few scattered homesteads. For a town of such historical importance, Oxford's is a very late entry on the scroll of English history.

The Romans had long gone and the westward expansion of the Saxons had pushed the Britons into Wales and Cornwall before the place where oxen forded the Thames – also close to present-day Folly Bridge – acquired the name which is now famous throughout the world. In about AD700, legend has it, Frideswide, the daughter of a local chieftain, was pursued to this ford by Algar, king of the Mercian Saxons. Algar had attempted to force his attentions on to the virginal, pious and distinctly reluctant Frideswide and, catching her by the river, he was intent on doing the same again – with as much force as was required. But, before Algar could complete his conquest a thunderbolt blinded him. Recognizing this as a sign from heaven, Algar asked Frideswide's forgiveness. This she granted and his sight was immediately restored. King Algar disappears from the pages of history, but Frideswide, as St Frideswide, lives on in the name of a monastery built for her by her father. St Frideswide is said to have died in her monastery in 727.

If there is any truth to the legend, then it is thought that St Frideswide's monastery stood on the site now occupied by Christ Church, the monastery church lying beneath what is now the cathedral. Excavations having shown that from about 780 there was a settlement close by. It is not until 900 that Oxford is first mentioned, appearing then in a list of thirty-two *burhs* (literally 'fortresses', but actually well-defended towns) which Alfred the Great set up as part of a defensive system against incursions by the Danes. Alfred died in 899, but his system was taken up by his son and successor, Edward the Elder, and more particularly by his daughter, Aethelfled. Aethelfled, known as the 'Lady of the Mercians', is thought to have been responsible for laying down the basic grid-pattern of Saxon Oxford. It was now an important place, its spectacular rise to prominence due not only to its being a burh, but to its position on the border between Mercia and Wessex. The marriage of Aethelred, the Mercian king, and Aethelfled may have brought peace, but it was an uneasy one, particularly as Wessex remained free of Danish control while Mercia was still subject to incursions from the north.

By 1000 the constant Viking attacks on England had created the peculiar situation that while the Saxon and Viking lords fought for control of the country and the peasant class of both sides played out their destiny as battle fodder, the merchant classes traded more or less amicably. By 1002 Oxford was a Saxon town, but outside the walls lived a number of Danish traders. They were wealthy, probably conspicuously so, and on 13 November the Saxon townsfolk attacked them. The attack was savage, fuelled by years of fear of Viking raiders and, no doubt, a loathing of well-heeled foreigners. The Danes sought sanctuary in the town church, but in an act of sacrilege it was set alight, the Danes dying in its ashes. The Saxon king, Aethelred the Unready, compen-

Carfax Tower

sated the town for the loss of its church, adding an extra dimension to the fury of the Danes, though it was not until 1009 that they organized a revenge attack, sailing up the Thames and sacking the city. They repeated the raid in 1015, the year before Aethelred's death and Cnut's conquest of England. With Cnut in control, a Danish army was stationed at Oxford.

The Norman Conquest meant that Oxford lost its importance as a border town and, despite the building of a castle within five years of the Conquest by the Norman lord Robert D'Oilly, the city went into a decline which lasted almost a hundred years. It then grew in importance, in part because of its position close to the Cotswolds. In early medieval England the Cotswolds were the most important area of the country, the sheep that thrived there – known as Cotswold Lions – producing a wool so valuable that traders travelled from Tuscany to buy fleeces. Standing at the edge of the Cotswolds – and at the heart of southern England – Oxford became a centre for the wool and woollen cloth trades, using the water – for power and washing – of the Thames. By the late 13th century Oxford was the third most important city in the country after London and York.

Parks Road

But there was another reason for the city's rise: its importance as a centre of learning. Despite the considerable efforts of historians, it has not been possible to identify the date of founding of Oxford's university. It is likely that only the Sorbonne is older amongst European universities, and it is possible that a dispute between Henry II of England and Louis VII which led to the expulsion of English students from Paris led to the founding of Oxford. In 1122 St Frideswide's monastery had been refounded as an Augustinian house, and the order opened a second house (Osney Abbey) a few years later. Monasteries were centres of learning in medieval England and so it is likely that there were already students in the town when the Sorbonne exiles arrived. In 1221 the first Chancellor of Oxford University was appointed, although there was an association of clerks (as students were then called) several years earlier, probably around 1200.

In 1209 a local woman was murdered. The men of the town sought out two students and lynched them, though historians believe it unlikely that they were guilty of the killing. Other students, fearing for their lives, left in fear, travelling to Cambridge where they helped the founding of the university which is still Oxford's main rival. The remaining students were given protection by the King, who also fined the town for the lynching, so recognition of the university was granted before the appointment of the first Chancellor made it official.

The early students lived in Academic Halls which were run by graduates who charged for bed and board, and teaching. The Halls were independent of, but licensed and supervised by, the University. Soon some of the rich monastic houses of England, and some of the country's bishops (whose land holdings made them as rich as the monasteries), were creating their own centres of learning in the town. These centres were called colleges and over the years the independent halls were absorbed into the colleges, or closed down, or themselves became colleges. Only in 1976 did St Edmund Hall become a college.

Though the expanding University created one of the world's great seats of learning and brought some wealth to the town, the relationship between what is now called 'Town and Gown' was never an easy one. The rich and powerful institutions that created the colleges often did so at the expense of the townsfolk, commandeering the land or property it needed for building, leaving the evicted tenants to survive as best they could. With the wool industry in decline, such survival was frequently in abject poverty, fostering resentment. On St Scholastica's Day in 1355, a group of students at the Swyndelstock Tavern at Carfax (in the centre of the town) became involved in an argument with the landlord. History does not record the reason for the argument, but it rapidly became heated. Blows were exchanged and a number of townsfolk came to the support of the landlord. Within minutes the resentment of ages welled up and a riot broke out. For several days a mob of Oxford men attacked the colleges, beating up students, many of whom died of their injuries. When things eventually calmed down the King ordered that the town's mayor and council should pay reparations to the University, and until the middle of the 19th century an annual ceremony was held at St Mary's Church at which the council handed over an old penny for every student who died, a humiliating act which did nothing to ease the turbulent relationship between Town and Gown.

The townsfolk of Oxford were long-suffering: not only did they feel themselves second-class citizens in their own town, but the wool industry declined, the town was the victim of catastrophic fires at regular intervals, and then, in 1348, Black Death killed a third of the population – though the plague infected townsfolk and students alike. But things did improve, both for the city and the University. Henry VIII's dissolution of the monasteries meant that many of the colleges became rich overnight. The University expanded and the money it spent on providing itself with piped water and improved sewage systems also benefited the town. By 1642 Oxford was again one of England's most important cities, and when the Civil War broke out in that year the King, seeking a headquarters away from Parliament's stronghold of London and the south-east, chose the town. The King held a parliament in Christ Church Hall and his forces distributed themselves throughout the surrounding area, occupying the towns of Henley, Marlow and Reading in the Chilterns, and Marlborough, Hungerford and Newbury on the chalk downlands.

Merton Street

Oxford itself, perhaps unsurprisingly, was divided, the University enthusiastically supporting the King, while the town supported (but more quietly) Parliament. Oxford was not attacked and, before his final defeat, the King fled the city. Perhaps to the amazement of the townsfolk, following Charles' execution Oliver Cromwell was made Chancellor of the University, though after the Restoration Charles II was warmly welcomed by both town and University when he visited.

After the Civil War Oxford's development followed that of other British cities. A canal linking the city to Birmingham opened in 1790 and the railway arrived in 1850. Then, in the early years of the 20th century, William Richard Morris began to repair bicycles in a shed in the garden of his parents' house in Cowley. Morris had been born in Worcester, but his parents were from Oxford and moved back to the city when William was still very young. The young Morris had left school at 14 and was apprenticed to a bicycle repairman, but soon set up on his own, working from the garden shed. From the shed he moved to his own repair shop in the High Street. Here he began to make, as well as repair, bicycles, then moved on to making and repairing motor cycles.

He soon began to repair motor cars too, opening the Oxford Garage in Longwall Street, close to the old city walls. Within a few years he was making motor cars, moving production to newer premises at Cowley. The Morris make of car became one of Britain's biggest sellers, and one of its most distinctive, the famous curved radiators earning them the nickname 'Bullnose Morrises'. Later, the names of both Oxford and Cowley were commemorated in particular models.

Morris' enterprise brought other industries to Oxford, the city growing in prosperity. The Morris car company took over Wolseley and Riley, and created the first million-selling car, the Morris Minor. Morris himself disliked the design (by Alec Issigonis, who later designed the Mini), claiming the car looked like a poached egg. In 1952 Morris amalgamated with Austin to produce the British Motor Company. Today the Morris works at Cowley is the home of Rover.

William Morris was knighted in 1928 and ennobled in 1938 for his services to the country and his charitable works. On his elevation to the peerage he took the name Viscount Nuffield, Nuffield being the small village – mid-way between Wallingford and Henley-on-Thames – where he lived. The original Morris Garage also became famous, though not everyone now recognizes that it gave its name – or, rather, its initials, MG – to a sporty version of Morris' cars designed by his garage manager, Cecil Kimber. In 1958 Lord Nuffield founded Nuffield College, a post-graduate college: he died in 1963 at the age of 85.

The University

Oxford University is a federation of forty-one independent colleges who choose their own students and provide those students with tutors (called dons). The colleges are self-supporting, some being extremely rich, while the University provides central libraries and laboratories, sets the courses to be studied, sets and marks examinations and awards degrees. The University also employs lecturers (in addition to the college tutors), student education being a mixture of (non-compulsory) lectures and (compulsory) tutorials. Oxford introduced degrees for woman in 1920 (and proudly notes that its rival, Cambridge, did not do so until

Christ Chruch College Garden

1948), though there had been female colleges since 1878 when Lady Margaret Hall (named for Henry VII's mother) was founded. Its first head was Elizabeth Wordsworth, the grand-niece of William. Elizabeth Wordsworth also founded St Hugh's (the fifth female college) in 1886. During the second half of the 20th century single-sex colleges were seen as politically incorrect: today all undergraduate colleges are mixed apart from St Hilda's – founded in 1893 by Dorothea Beale, Principal of Cheltenham Ladies' College – which remains female only. There are about 15,000 students, the population of Oxford being about 120,000.

Exploring the City

It could be argued that the title should read 'Exploring the University', as the colleges comprise the majority of Oxford's attractions. Some writers have used this fact to denigrate the city, seeing the undoubted elitism and the rituals of the academic world as a reminder of the British class system. While such arguments have merit – how much merit being entirely dependent upon the position you choose to take – it is no fault of the buildings. Oxford is unquestionably one of the most architecturally and historically interesting cities in Britain, a magical place where the quiet of ancient quadrangles can be found just yards from noisy modernity. Oxford is also very compact, most of the worthwhile sights being a matter of minutes' walk from Carfax, a conveniently central spot. But to see all those worthwhile sights in one walk the visitor would need a good pair of walking legs and be resigned to merely glancing at the best features. Here we present four short walks: completion of them all will allow the visitor to really see the city. The walks can, of course, be combined, but to enjoy, as well as see, Oxford it is necessary to take your time.

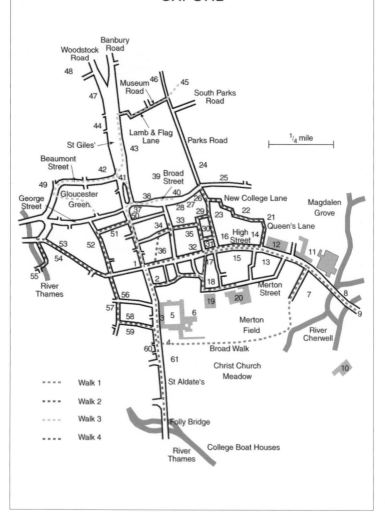

Key to the Walks

Walk 1

1 Carfax Tower
2 Museum of Oxford
3 Tom Tower
4 War Memorial Gardens
5 Christ Church
6 Cathedral
7 Botanic Gardens
8 Magdalen Bridge
9 The Plain
10 St Hilda's College
11 Magdalen College
12 St Edmund Halll
13 Examination Schools
14 Queen's College
15 University College
16 All Souls College
17 Rhodes Building
18 Oriel College
19 Corpus Christi College
20 Merton College

Walk 2

21 St Peter-in-the-East
      Church
22 New College
23 Hertford College
24 Wadham College
25 Holywell Music Room
26 Clarendon Building
27 Sheldonian Theatre
28 Museum of
      the History of Science
29 Bodleian Library/
      School of Divinity
30 Radcliffe Camera
31 St Mary's Church
32 Brasenose College
33 Exeter College
34 Jesus College
35 Lincoln College
36 Covered Market

Walk 3

37 Oxford Story
38 Balliol College
39 Trinity College
40 Blackwell's
41 Martyrs' Memorial
42 Ashmolean Museum
43 St John's College
44 Regents Park College
45 University Museum/
      Pitt-Rivers Museum
46 Keble College
47 St Benet's Hall
48 Somerville College
49 Worcester College

Walk 4

50 St Michael's Church
51 Oxford Union
52 St Peter's College
53 Nuffield College
54 Oxford Castle
55 Morrells Brewery
56 Museum of Modern Art
57 St Ebbe's Church
58 Pembroke College
59 Campion Hall
60 Alice's Shop
61 Bate Collection

Walk 1: Christ Church and High Street

Carfax takes its name from the Latin *quadri furcus*, four-forked, as it was the crossing point of the main streets in the medieval town, a fact which made it the busy heart of old Oxford. It is still the busiest place in town, the pedestrianizing of Queen Street and limit on access to Cornmarket Street still allowing a ribbon of traffic to stretch along St Aldate's and High Street. Carfax is actually the name of the road junction, but is also applied to the tower on the north-western corner. The tower is all that remains of St Martin's Church. The first church on the site was built in the early 10th century and became the headquarters of the townsfolk during the riots of 1355. It is said that the students assembled in St Mary's Church in the High Street and that the two factions would then march towards each other to do battle. This confrontation, set up in the best traditions of the Hollywood Western, would seem comical were it not for the deaths that occurred.

In 1818 the old church was demolished and replaced, but the new church lasted only eighty years before it, too, was demolished to make way for road widening. Only the tower survived the demolition. It is 22m (72ft) high, ninety-nine steps taking the visitor to a superb viewpoint of the nearby colleges. The clock face on the eastern (High Street) side of the tower has two 'quarter boys' who strike the quarter hours.

Quarter Boys, Carfax Tower

From Carfax head southward along St Aldate's, passing the neo-Jacobean Town Hall, built in the 1890s, on the left to reach the **Museum of Oxford**, also on the left. The museum is housed in the old city library, built at the same time as the Town Hall. The entrance is around the corner in Blue Boar Lane, named for an old inn, demolished to make way for the library. In the museum the history of the city, including the Morris car company, is explored with the help of some very interesting items, including a model of Oxford Castle made by prisoners held there and – more macabre than interesting – the skeleton of Giles Covington who was hanged for murder in 1791.

Continuing down St Aldate's – the main Post Office is to the right – the great gatehouse to Christ Church College is reached on the left. This is **Tom Tower**, its lower section built by Cardinal Thomas Wolsey when he founded the college (as Cardinal College) in 1525; the upper part was built by Sir Christopher Wren in 1681. The gatehouse is named for Great Tom, the bell which hangs in it. Interestingly the bell is named not for Wolsey, but for St Thomas à Becket. The bell originally hung in Osney Abbey but was sequestered when the abbey was dissolved by Henry VIII. It was recast before being hung in Wren's tower. The bell weighs 7 tons and each night at 9.05pm it rings 101 times to commemorate the first scholars of the college. The curious timing of the chimes is another Oxford tradition: the college lies five minutes to the west of the Greenwich Meridian and so the chiming begins at 9pm 'Oxford Time'. Anciently, the chiming also signalled the closing of the college gates: students arriving after this time were required to pay to gain access to their rooms.

Visitors are not allowed through the gatehouse of Tom Tower, so continue along St Aldate's to reach the **War Memorial Gardens** and Broad Walk on the left. The Gardens were laid out in 1925 to commemorate those from Christ Church who died in the 1914–18 War. Follow Broad Walk, soon reaching the Meadow Buildings on the left, where there is access to **Christ Church**, arguably the finest of the University's colleges, and certainly the one occupying the best position, overlooking the water meadows – Christ Church Meadow – that lie between the two Oxford rivers, the Thames and the Cherwell. The tour of Christ Church is a short, but essential, detour from our walk.

Christ Church was founded (as Cardinal College) by Thomas Wolsey, but refounded in 1546 as Christ Church after the Cardinal's fall from power. (Henry VIII renamed the college after himself in 1532, following Wolsey's fall in 1529, but refounded it when the college chapel was made the cathedral church of the new Oxford diocese – this is the only university college chapel in the world to be a cathedral.)

Visitors entering Christ Church follow a trail – a deviation from which can be brought to your attention in no uncertain manner by the bowler-hatted 'Bulldogs' who patrol the grounds with the express intention of living up to their name – which takes you to the cloisters of the earlier abbey which Wolsey sequestered when founding his college. To make way for Tom Quad, Wolsey demolished part of the cloisters as well as several bays of the cathedral. The enclosed cloisters, with their pretty windows, are 15th century, contemporary with sections of the cathedral, though much of that is older, dating to the 12th century when it was the church of the new Augustinian monastery of St Frideswide. The cathedral is the smallest in Britain and is said to house the remains of the saint,

Christ Church Gardens from the War Memorial Gardens

under a black marble slab to the north of the choir. The choir is one of the highlights of the building, its ceiling magnificently vaulted. The main highlight is the stained glass, including a series of superb windows by the pre-Raphaelite artists. The windows of St Lucy Chapel are 14th century and include a very rare depiction of the martyrdom of St Thomas à Becket. Henry VIII ordered all monuments of Becket to be destroyed – here only Becket's head was removed. The Latin Chapel has a window by Edward Burne-Jones depicting scenes from the life of St Frideswide – including a startling rendering of the blinding of King Algar – while the St Catherine Window to the east of the choir depicts Edith Liddell (sister of the Alice of *Alice in Wonderland*) as the saint. This window is by Burne-Jones and William Morris (the pre-Raphaelite artist and leading figure of the Arts and Crafts Movement rather than the car builder).

From the cloister a stairway beneath a fine vaulted ceiling leads to the largest pre-Victorian hall in the University. The hall's hammerbeam roof is superb, and the sense of the hall being a special place is heightened by the portrait of Henry VIII and those of former students, thirteen of whom became Prime Ministers of Britain. There is also a portrait of Charles Dodgson, a mathematics lecturer at the college (having been a student there too). He was a shy man, having been a shy boy surrounded by seven sisters, and found the company of children easier than that of adults. He made friends with Alice and Edith Liddell, the young daughters of the college's Dean, taking them on boat trips and country walks during which he invented stories. The stories were eventually published in 1865 as *Alice's Adventures in Wonderland*. In the book various locations in Oxford can be identified by knowledgeable readers: the Cheshire cat was Alice Liddell's tabby Dinah and the Red Queen was based on the sisters' governess, a strict, humourless woman. Dodgson published the book under the pseudonym Lewis Carroll: it was beautifully illustrated by the artist John Tenniel.

Dodgson published a sequel (*Through the Looking Glass*) in 1871 and a famous book of nonsense verse, *The Hunting of the*

Snark, in 1876. His friendship with Alice Liddell ended when she grew up: she married a Christ Church student when she was 19 and moved to the New Forest. Dodgson left the college in 1881 at the age of 49 and died in 1898, aged 66. He never married.

From the hall the route for visitors leads to Tom Quad which, at about 80m square (actually 264ft x 261ft, not quite square) is the largest of any college. Wolsey completed three sides of the Quad, the northern side being completed – to the same design – by John Fell, the College Dean who also commissioned Wren to add the top section to Tom Tower. At the Quad's north-eastern corner is Fell Tower, built in 1876 but named for John Fell, whose statue stands close by. The main statue in the Quad is of Mercury, a copy of Giovanni da Bologna's original, standing on a plinth by Edward Lutyens.

Go under Fell Tower to reach Kilcanon, on the left, named for the winter's wind which swirls colder here than elsewhere, cold enough to mortify the clergy! Also on the left is Blue Boar Quad, its main buildings forming the southern edge of Blue Boar Lane. There are also two further quads: Peckwater, named for an inn that was demolished to make room for it, and the smaller Canterbury. The southern edge of Peckwater Quad is formed by New Library, dating from 1772 and with impressive Corinthian columns. In Canterbury Quad is the **Christ Church Picture Gallery**, with an impressive collection of paintings and drawings, some as early as the 14th century. There are several priceless works – including paintings by Veronese and Tintoretto – but in pride of place is the portrait of Henry VIII, almost certainly the work of Holbein. The Picture Gallery has its own entrance from Oriel Square for those not wishing to make the full tour of Christ Church.

The tour of Christ Church must exit from Canterbury Quad into Merton Street, detouring from the suggested walk. To regain that, go past Corpus Christi College, to the right, and turn right along Merton Grove (with Merton College on the left), passing Dead Man's Walk (so named because it was once the route of funerals to the Jewish burial ground, now the Botanic Gardens), on the left, to regain Broad Walk.

The suggested walk continues along Broad Walk, soon reaching New Walk, to the right. This leads to the River Thames and its boathouses, and was the route often taken by Lewis Carroll and Alice Liddell. Broad Walk now follows the edge of Christ Church Meadow, on the right. Though grazed, this has never been cultivated and is a haven for wildflowers and insects. It is a true water meadow, often flooding (and occasionally freezing) in winter. Gilbert White, famous as the author of *The Natural History of Selbourne* was one who studied the plants on the Meadow.

When the River Cherwell (pronounced Charwell in another of Oxford's idiosyncrasies) is reached, bear left to reach Rose Lane. Soon, to the right, an entrance to the **Botanic Gardens** is reached. Founded in 1621 as the Physicke Garden for the School of Medicine, this was the first botanic garden in Britain (and only the third in Europe after Pisa and Leyden). The garden was created on the site of the town's Jewish burial grounds, the ground level being raised to avoid repeated flooding from the nearby River Cherwell. The raising was by the application of soil, and several thousand loads of 'mucke' and 'dunge' – which begs the question of the difference between muck and dung. The 3-acre garden was then enclosed by a $4\frac{1}{4}$m (14ft) wall to protect the plants. The wall still exists on three sides, the fourth now completed by a laboratory. Under the watchful eyes of the first keepers, Jacob Bobart, a German who was succeeded by his son, the pair

Christ Church College

keeping the garden for seventy-seven years, a plant collection of over a thousand species was built up. Today it is supplemented by huge glasshouses full of tropical and sub-tropical species including many crop plants: bananas, sugar, tea and coffee. The main gardens, laid out formally around a central pond, are a delight and the view of Magdalen College's tower beyond the flower beds and specimen trees is alone worth the visit.

The Gardens have an entrance/exit on to High Street which Pevsner described as 'one of world's great streets'. Turn right to reach **Magdalen Bridge** over the River Cherwell. The river is lovely here and walks along the bank, and punting on the water, are very popular – punts are available for hire. The first bridge here was built of wood in 1002. It was replaced by a stone bridge in the 16th century, but this was itself replaced by a drawbridge when Oxford was the Royalist HQ during the Civil War. The present bridge dates from 1772, though it was widened in 1882. Across the bridge is The Plain, a busy cross-roads with a fountain provided, in 1899, by Morrells Brewery as a drinking trough for horses. Bearing right here is the Iffley Road. On its running track on 6 May 1954 Roger (now Sir Roger) Bannister became the first man to break the four-minute barrier for the mile. Chris Brasher, one of his pace-makers that day and later on Olympic gold medalist – the other pace-maker was Chris (now Sir Christopher) Chataway – has since noted that the run was watched by about two thousand people and that he had met all ten thousand of them during later years. Close to The Plain is **St Hilda's College**, founded in 1893 by Dorothea Beale, the famous Principal of Cheltenham Ladies College. Begun as a college for women students, it is now the only all-women college at Oxford.

Across from the Botanic Gardens is **Magdalen College**. The college, pronounced 'Maudlin', was founded in 1458 by William of Waynflate, one-time Bishop of Winchester, then Lord Chancellor under Henry VI. As it was built outside the old city walls, space was not a limitation, this helping the founder to create one of the most beautiful of all the city's colleges. The most striking feature is the bell tower. At 6am on May morning (always 1 May

– the date does not change, unlike the public holiday) the college choristers sing madrigals from the top of the tower. The tradition is thought to date from the tower's completion in 1505. In the early days it is likely that few listened to the choir, but today the singing brings out a crowd and heralds a day of events, most of them impromptu: Morris men dance in the High Street, the local cafés do a roaring trade and champagne breakfasts are enjoyed on the banks of (and punts on) the Cherwell.

The tower was used as a look-out during the Civil War, but the college became anti-Royalist when James II tried to force Magdalen to become a Catholic seminary. The attempt soon failed, the return of the college fellows still being celebrated as Restoration Day on 25 October. Historically Magdalen has been an arts- rather than sports- or science-oriented college: former students include Oscar Wilde and Sir John Betjeman.

After enjoying the college's gargoyles, the visitor enters the college from High Street, reaching St John's Quad, which has an external pulpit still used for a sermon on the Sunday closest to St John the Baptist's Day (24 June), a tradition dating from the founding. The college chapel is reached beyond Muniment Tower, both dating from about 1485. The chapel has some good carved figures and holds the monument tomb of Richard Patten,

Punts near Magdalen Bridge

the father of the founder, who died in 1450. The Quad's other tower is Founder's Tower, the original college entrance, which leads to the cloisters – now Cloister Quad – the original centre of the college. With its wisteria and figured buttresses it is a delight: the visitor could hardly guess that the north and east wings were rebuilt in the 19th century after a (thankfully) failed attempt to demolish them to make way for new buildings. The New Buildings (not too imaginatively named, but the age – about 270 years – gives an idea of Magdalen's antiquity) are the only completed section of a planned new quad. To the left as you approach is the fenced edge of Magdalen Grove, a deer park. The park provided venison for the college and apparently still does on occasions, deer often being seen by visitors. To the right a path leads to a bridge over the River Cherwell. Beyond, Addison's Walk, a tree-lined path, follows a curious loop of the Cherwell around a pleasant area of water meadow. The name commemorates Joseph Addison (1672–1719) whose room at Magdalen overlooked the Cherwell water meadows. Addison was a poet and essayist, whose essays in the *Spectator* in praise of nature rather than man's attempt to create formal gardens was responsible for the change to naturalistic parks and gardens.

Return along High Street, passing the Botanic Gardens and Rose Lane to the left. The next turn right is Longwall Street which follows the line of the old city wall. Along the street – on the left, just before St Cross Road is reached on the right – is the site of William Morris' Oxford Garage. The nearby Eastgate Hotel marks the site of the east gate through the old wall. Beyond, to the right, is **St Edmund Hall**, which was a hall until 1976 when it achieved college status. The hall has a claim to being the oldest of Oxford's educational establishments, perhaps dating to 1190 when, it is believed, Edmund of Abingdon taught here. Edmund was canonized in 1248, but the hall he had created eventually passed to Queen's College, and then to Oriel before becoming independent. Opposite St Edmund Hall are the **Examination Schools**, where students sit their finals. For their exams the students are required to wear *subfuge* : dark suit, white shirt and bow tie for men; dark skirt, white blouse and black tie for women. Just beyond, and opposite Queen's Lane, on the right, No. 84 High Street was the site of Frank Cooper's grocery shop. Here, his wife made the first marmalade bearing the Cooper name. It proved so popular that demand outran the supply from the family kitchen and a factory was set up. Though the Cooper family sold out long ago, Cooper's marmalade is still made and sold worldwide.

Front Quad
Queen's College

To the right, beyond Queens Lane, is **Queen's College**, founded in 1340 by Robert de Eglesfeld, the chaplain to Edward III's wife, Queen Philippa, and named in her honour. Despite the naming for Philippa the statue at the main gate is not her, but George III's wife, Queen Carolina, who gave money for the rebuilding of much of the college in the 18th century. In fact, despite the 14th century foundation, nothing remains that is earlier than 17th century. Beyond the High Street's narrow baroque façade is Front Quad, which Pevsner claimed to be 'the grandest piece of classical architecture in Oxford'. The Quad, part of Queen Carolina's beneficence, is in English baroque style. Beyond Front Quad is North Quad, the older of the two by about a century. Queen's has two strange traditions, each celebrated by a dinner. That commemorating the founder involves each guest being given a needle and thread, a play on Eglesfeld's name, a needle and thread in the courtly French of the day being *aiguille et fils*. The second dinner is the Boar's Head Feast which is claimed to commemorate a student surviving an attack by a wild boar by being quick-witted enough to push his copy of Aristotle's *Politics* down the animal's throat. The boar choked to death, which some might see as a comment on the digestibility of Aristotle's philosophy.

Just beyond Queen's is the High Street's famous sycamore tree, the only feature which can be seen from both ends of the street.

Directly opposite is **University College**, Oxford's oldest college. Legend has it that it was first founded by Alfred the Great in the early 9th century, but there is scant support for this and some support for it being a hoax theory. It certainly dates from 1249 when William of Durham, who had left the Sorbonne for Oxford along with the others, gave money for buying the first hall. All the present buildings date from the 17th/early 18th century, and at that time a statue of King Alfred was replaced by one of Queen Anne. There is another statue to Queen Mary and also one of James II, portraying him in a toga. The statue is one of only two which survive in Britain of this unpopular king. The college has two fine quads, Front and Radcliffe. A passage in the north-west corner of Front Quad reaches a more expressive statue set beneath a dome. It is of the naked, drowned body of the poet Percy Bysshe Shelley lying on a plinth supported by winged lions. In front the Muse of Poetry holds her head in grief. The poet had been a student at the college for just six months when in 1811, after jointly authoring a pamphlet entitled *The Necessity of Atheism*, he was expelled. The monument was sculpted by Edward Onslow Ford, for the poet's grave in Rome (he had been drowned near Livorno when the boat he was travelling in sank in a storm) but was found to be too big. The college's chapel has some beautiful 17th century stained glass by the German artist Abraham von Linge; many believe it to be the finest of his work.

University College lies beyond Logic Lane, named for a college for philosophers which once stood beside it. On the other side of the college – beyond the Shelley Memorial whose dome is clearly visible from the street – are a collection of beautiful 18th century buildings reaching to Magpie Lane. Opposite these fine buildings is All Souls College and Catte Street which leads to the most impressive part of the University (*see* Walk 2).

All Souls College was co-founded by Henry VI and Archbishop Henry Chichele in 1437 as a memorial to the men killed at Agincourt. It is the only college never to have had undergraduate students, being a research college with one of the University's finest libraries; to be made a Fellow of All Souls is considered to the highest academic honour the University can bestow on an individual. The High Street façade is original and has a lovely entranceway with statues of the founders and carvings of souls in Purgatory and on Resurrection Day. The entrance leads to the Front Quad, also original, and on to the later North Quad, which can be accessed from Catte Street. The North Quad is by Nicholas Hawksmoor and houses the Codrington Library. By the 16th and 17th centuries the position of All Souls in the University hierarchy had fallen, with Fellowships being bought and sold and the Fellows acquiring a reputation more for drunkenness and dubious deals than for scholarship. In 1710 Christopher Codrington, a Fellow who was a member of the rich West Indian sugar family – he was also Governor of the Leeward Islands – left a fortune in his will and his huge collection of books to the college. The North Quad was built, the Codrington Library opened and the college's reputation restored. The library is only open to visitors by prior appointment. It is housed in the Quad's northern side, but the eastern side is more impressive, with twin towers in soaring Gothic style. The Quad's large sundial is believed to be by Sir Christopher Wren, who was the college bursar at the time of its construction. The college's real treasure lies in the chapel: a phenomenal reredos in Spanish Gothic style carefully restored by Sir George Gilbert Scott.

Across Catte Street is St Mary's Church which, though it fronts on to High Street, is so much a part of Radcliffe Square that it is considered on Walk 2. Opposite is the **Rhodes Building** of Oriel College, built with money left to the college by Cecil Rhodes, a former student. Rhodes, who made his fortune in Southern Africa as one of the founders of the De Beers diamond company, gave his name to Rhodesia (now Zambia and Zimbabwe) and created a fund for the granting of Rhodes Scholarships which allow gifted students from overseas to study at Oxford. Rhodes, who died in 1902 aged just 49, stipulated that scholars should not necessarily be academically brilliant but should have high ability in a particular field. They could, therefore, be athletes or show qualities of leadership or great character. About seventy scholarships are

Front Quad, Corpus Christi College

awarded annually, about half of them to students from the USA – President Bill Clinton was a Rhodes Scholar.

A good detour now turns left along Oriel Street, but before going that way we continue along High Street. To the left, both before and after King Edward Street, are an array of lovely buildings, mostly dating from the 18th and 19th centuries, though some incorporate early sections. No. 116 is the shop of the Oxford University Press, while the National Westminster Bank (Nos. 120/121) has a superb neo-Gothic façade dating from 1866. **No.**

126 has the best 17th century façade in Oxford, three storeys, part-timbered and with curved bays. A little further on, down a narrow alley, is **Kemp Hall**, built in 1637 by a local alderman. With its gables, wooden door, projecting canopy and mullioned windows it is a delight. On the left side of the street it is now only a short step to Carfax.

On the right side, opposite King Edward Street, is Brasenose College whose entrance is in Radcliffe Square (*see* Walk 2). Beyond Turl Street is **The Mitre** whose cellars date to the 13th century, though the above-ground building is 17th century. In its earliest days it was an inn, a favourite spot for students. Later it was a coaching inn. Today the tradition is maintained with a restaurant/tea shop. Beyond The Mitre, the buildings are, largely, 19th century remodels of earlier façades.

The suggested detour turns left along Oriel Street to reach Oriel Square and the main entrance of **Oriel College**. The college was founded in 1326 and takes its name from a house, La Oriole – named for its upper bay window, a form now called an oriel window – which the college acquired in 1329. That house, and all the other medieval parts of the college, were lost in a major rebuild in the 16th century. This rebuild produced the superb Front Quad which fronts on to Oriel Square. The Quad's stairway to the hall has the inscription *Regnante Carolo* (Charles reigns) above it, an uncompromising statement of support for Charles I at the time of the Civil War (which began as work on the college was being completed). Towards High Street there are two further quads, Back and St Mary's, the latter completed by the Rhodes Building.

From Oriel Square, bear left along Merton Street, passing **Corpus Christi College** on your left. The college was founded in 1517 by Richard Foxe, Bishop of Winchester, and is one of the smallest in the University. It is also one of the loveliest, the 16th century Front Quad being simple, but wonderfully elegant. At its centre is a sundial dating from 1581. At the top is the college's emblem, the pelican. In the 16th century it was believed (wrongly) that the pelican pulled feathers from her breast to feed her young on blood: this was seen as a symbol of Christ's sacrifice.

Corpus Christi College

At the base of the pillar is a perpetual calendar dating from 1606. The college chapel has an altarpiece once thought to be the work of Rubens, but now thought to be by a pupil of the master, and a brass eagle lectern dating from 1537, the oldest of any Oxford College. Close to the chapel is Fellows' Quad, the smallest in Oxford. It is closed, on the southern side, by Fellows' Building behind which is a lovely garden from which there is a view across Christ Church Meadow.

Richard Foxe, the founder, was a friend of Erasmus, and held similar 'radical' views. He therefore insisted on the study of Latin and Greek works which were seen, at the time, as pagan as they pre-dated Christianity. In this respect Foxe can be seen as embracing the Renaissance, which was then at its height in Italy. In 1963 the college also admitted women to its hall as dining guests, an equally radical move for the time, though it did not follow this up by being the first college to become mixed.

Further along Merton Street is **Merton College**, a complete contrast to Corpus Christi, being one of Oxford's largest colleges and almost as grand as Christ Church. It was founded in 1264 by Walter de Merton, the Lord Chancellor, and has sections dating from that time. Mob Quad is 14th century, the oldest of all Oxford's quadrangles. The quad is reached through a gate tower which has recent statues of Walter de Merton and Henry III. The carving above the entrance is much older and shows St John the

Baptist or, perhaps, Christ in the wilderness. Beyond the gateway is Front Quad, rebuilt in 1874. From the Quad a passage under Fitzjames Arch leads to the 17th century Fellows' Quad. The arch was built in the late 15th century by Robert Fitzjames, the college warden who was interested in astrology and had the signs of the zodiac carved on the arch bosses

Mob Quad – the name is a mystery – is reached from Fellows' or Front Quad. On its southern side is the college library which has original reading desks, still with the chains that secured valu-

Mob Quad, Merton College

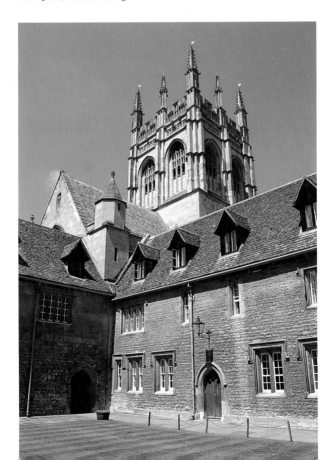

able manuscripts. Many experts believe that Merton's is the finest medieval library to have survived. In addition to the chained desks the library has locked chests for storing manuscripts (a feature which pre-dates books, and, therefore, bookshelves), an astrolabe, an instrument used for measuring the angle of elevation of stars which is believed to have been owned by Chaucer, and one of the first Bibles to have been printed in Welsh. The library windows contain 15th century glass. Some of the glass in the college chapel is even older, perhaps dating from the late 13th century. The oldest is in the East Window. Completed by glass from the 15th/16th centuries, the window is one of the finest in Oxford.

Adjacent to the library, the Max Beerbohm Room has a collection of drawings by Sir Max, who was a Merton scholar. Beerbohm's *Zuleika Dobson* is a satire on Oxford student life, the heroine of the title breaking the heart of everyone she meets. A rather more serious author (usually, if not exclusively), T.S. Eliot, was also a Merton man.

Opposite the college is Postmaster's Hall, part of Merton. The name is confusing as it has nothing to do with the postal service, being derived from 'portionist', the name given to Merton's poorest students (who required a portion of their expenses to be paid from other sources). Just beyond the hall is the entrance to Oxford's real tennis court. Real (from 'royal') tennis is played in a walled court with a net dividing the 'service' and 'hazard' halves of the court. A hard ball is used and rebounds from the walls are allowed. The game is said to have been invented by monks who played in the monastery cloisters, and was the forerunner of lawn tennis. The game declined in popularity because of the expense of creating courts. Visitors cannot use the court, but can visit the shop, where balls are still handmade.

From Merton College, return to Oriel Square and bear left along Bear Lane passing, to the right, the **Bear Inn**, one of Oxford's oldest, dating from the mid-13th century. It has one of the world's largest collections of club and regimental ties. Continue along Blue Boar Street, then turn right along St Aldate's to return to Carfax.

Walk 2: Around Radcliffe Square

From Carfax follow High Street past St Mary's Church and, just beyond Queen's College, turn left along the narrow Queen's Lane, passing the entrance to St Edmund Hall on the right. To the right where the lane turns sharp left is the **Church of St Peter-in-the-East**, whose architectural history is described by Pevsner as the most interesting in Oxford. The first church on the site was Saxon, raised in the 10th century. This was replaced in the following century, then incorporated into a Norman building. The crypt beneath the chancel dates from the 11th century and may be visited: ask at the Porter's Lodge of St Edmund Hall for the key. The rest of the church is closed to visitors as it now forms the library of St Edmund Hall. The students often use the shady churchyard for study, perhaps noticing that one of the headstones sits above the grave of James Sadler, the 'first English aeronaut'. On 4 October 1784 Sadler made the first hydrogen-filled balloon flight from Christ Church Meadow.

Continue along the lane, turning sharp left with it. You are now walking between New College to the right (look for the carved animals, the work of Michael Groser in the 1960s), and Queen's College, to the left. The lane turns right, goes under a 17th century arch and turns sharp left: to the right here is the entrance to **New College** founded in 1379 by William of Wykeham, the Bishop of Winchester, who founded Winchester College three years later. It is said that the Bishop founded the college to train a generation of clergymen. This was, as the college's statute puts it, to affect 'the fewness of the clergy, arising from pestilence, wars and other miseries', the Black Death having robbed the country of clerics and diplomats. The reason for the name was that Wykeham's college was the first to have been built from scratch, and so was 'new' rather than an incorporation/extension of existing buildings.

The entrance leads through the Gate Tower to the Great Quad which, though dating from the foundation, has been remodelled, a third storey having been added to three sides in 1674. The chapel is in fine Perpendicular style and has some excellent stained glass, much of it medieval. The great West Window was painted by Thomas Jarvis to a design by Sir Joshua Reynolds, though Reynolds was far from happy with the result. The work is historically interesting as Reynolds used Richard Brinsley Sheridan's wife as the model for the Virgin and other society ladies as models for the Virtues (described by one critic as looking like 'half-dressed, languishing harlots'). Beneath the window is a disturbing sculpture of Lazarus rising from the dead by Sir Jacob Epstein.

From the chapel the visitor can reach the cloisters, one of the highlights of the college. With the lovely windows and a dominating holm-oak, they are a haven of tranquillity. At the north-eastern corner of the Great Quad is the Muniment Tower from which a staircase leads to the hall. One of the portraits of former wardens is that of the Rev William Archibald Spooner (1844–1930), Warden from 1903, renowned for transposing the first letters or syllables of words to create 'Spoonerisms'. Some of these are authentic, such as his admonishment to a lazy student 'you have tasted two worms: you will leave by the town drain', to another student 'you have hissed your mystery lectures' and to a woman in church 'you are occupewing my pie', but others are probably apocryphal. Of the latter group, it would be very sad if the reverend gentlemen did not once propose a toast to 'our queer dean'.

From the Great Quad an archway leads to the Garden Quad where a fine wrought iron screen protects a fine garden. The curious mound is not part of an old defensive system, but a viewing platform for the garden. The section of wall is real, however, being a section of Oxford's old town wall. When William of Wykeham secured the land for his college, he agreed to maintain this section of the wall: every three years Oxford's Lord Mayor inspects the wall to ensure the agreement is being honoured.

Beyond New College's entrance, New College Lane threads a way between the Warden's House, on the left, and the cloister wall, on the right. Further along on the right, a plaque records Edmund Halley's house. Halley (1656–1742) was a student at

Bridge of Sighs, New College Lane

Queen's then, after discovering the comet which bears his name, was made a professor. The observatory he built on the house roof can still be seen. Go past St Helen's Passage, on the right, to reach the replica of Venice's Bridge of Sighs which links the two sections of **Hertford College**. The college entrance is in Catte Street – go under the bridge and turn left. Though not founded until 1740, Hertford stands on the site of Hart Hall which dated back to 1282 as an academic establishment. Its buildings date mainly from the 19th century.

A short detour is worthwhile here: turn right along Catte Street to the junction. Ahead is Parks Road with, to the right, **Wadham College**, founded in 1610 by Nicholas and Dorothy Wadham, wealthy Somerset landowners, and built, almost in its entirety, within three years. There are statues of the founders, and of James I, in the Front Quad. The chapel has some of Oxford's best 17th century stained glass: the East Window is by Bernard von Linge (brother of the more famous Abraham) and cost £114 on completion in 1622. Close by is the Fellows' Garden, a lovely spot where Christopher Wren, a student of Wadham, later met other leading scientists of the day to discuss the founding of the Royal Society. There is an equally fine garden in Back Quad, the gardens allowing you to forget that you are within a few steps of the heart of the University and the city centre.

Turning right at the junction takes the visitor into Holywell Street, one of Oxford's pleasantest streets, with many delightful buildings. Soon, on the left, the **Holywell Music Room** is reached. Now part of Wadham College, this mid-18th century building was the first purpose-built concert hall in England. It seats about 250 people and its regular programmes of recitals make it the oldest functioning concert hall in the world.

Passing beneath the Bridge of Sighs brings the visitor to the heart of the University. As you enter the assembly of buildings which is as close as Oxford gets to a campus, the **Clarendon Building** is to your right. This was built, in 1715, for the Oxford University Press (OUP), taking its name from Lord Clarendon whose account of the Civil War, *The History of the Great Rebellion*, had been a best-seller, making the OUP enough money to transfer from the basement and attic of the Sheldonian Theatre next door. The building, designed by Nicholas Hawksmoor, is now the University's Registry. The Clarendon's classical lines are completed by statues of the muses. Seven of these are the original lead statues, but two are recent fibreglass replacements.

More replacement statues can be seen by going between the Clarendon and the **Sheldonian Theatre** next door. In Broad Street the heads known as the Emperors gaze out across the road.

An 'Emperor',
Sheldonian Theatre

The original outsize heads were placed in front of the newly-built Sheldonian, but had eroded away by 1868. The replacements eroded even quicker and were replaced by new heads sculpted by the local sculptor Michael Black in 1972. The Sheldonian was commissioned by the University's then Chancellor, Gilbert Sheldon, in 1662 and designed by Christopher Wren (then only thirty and the University's Professor of Astronomy) who used a Roman theatre as his model. The theatre is remarkable for having an interior which is constructed almost entirely of wood. The 20m (60ft) ceiling is held aloft by huge beams: it was painted by Robert Streater, the work depicting the triumph of learning over vice. The theatre's final cupola can be visited: though the visitor is looking through glass the view is splendid. Sheldon built the Theatre for University functions, and it is still used for the annual ceremony where successful students receive their degrees, and for the 'Encaenia' where distinguished people receive honorary degrees. The Encaenia, held in June, includes a procession at which the Fellows of the University wear their colourful gowns.

Besides the Sheldonian, with an entrance in Broad Street, is the **Museum of the History of Science**, housed in the former Ashmolean Museum, a fine late 17th century building. The museum has a remarkable collection of early scientific instruments – astrolabes, sundials, chemical apparatus, microscopes and medical equipment – as well as a fine collection of watches, cameras, radios and gramophones. Among more endearing items is the blackboard used by Albert Einstein during his first Oxford lecture on relativity on 16 May 1931. It still has his chalked equations.

To the left as you go beneath the Bridge of Sighs are the **Bodleian Library** and **Divinity School**. The School was begun in 1420, but took almost seventy years to complete as funds for

School of Divinity

its construction kept running out. Its interior is said by many to be the finest in Oxford, especially for its vaulted ceiling, a lierne vault with a vast number (around 450) of bosses, each bearing a single word (many in Latin) so that groups generate phrases, or with coats-of-arms. Once used as an examination room for students, in 1554 the school was used for a very different form of trial when the Protestant bishops Cranmer, Latimer and Ridley were brought here for examination as heretics.

Above the schools is **Duke Humfrey's Library**, named for the younger brother of Henry V who donated his manuscripts to Oxford in 1440. The library, with its marvellous beamed ceiling, was opened to students in 1488, but within a few years had been made redundant by printing and, it is said, reduced in size by thefts carried out by Crown officials. A student of Magdalen, Thomas Bodley, became concerned at the lack of library facilities at Oxford and, as Elizabeth I's Dutch Ambassador, began a book collection which he eventually donated to the University. The library re-opened early in the 17th century, using Bodley's collection as its core of books. Some of these – leatherbound and priceless – can still be seen by visitors. The reason many volumes are stored with the spine away from the reader was to protect them from damage by the chains which secured them against theft.

In 1610 Bodley persuaded Stationer's Hall to send a copy of every new book to Oxford, one of only six libraries with such an agreement – and soon an extension to the library was required. One extension – known as the Selden End after John Selden, who donated the books for it – was added above the Convocation Hall in about 1650. The hall – at the western end of the Divinity School – was used for Royalist parliaments during the Civil War. As an aside, the Bodleian has always been a reference, rather than a lending, library and it is claimed that when Charles I asked to borrow a book during his Civil War stay he was politely, but firmly, refused.

The main extension, the **Old Schools Quadrangle**, which not only housed the Bodleian Library but was a home for the University's schools, is a wonderful place, the names of the various schools spelt out in gold above the doors. The Tower of Five Orders was built as a visual reference for students, the columns and capitals being – from the ground – Tuscan, Roman Doric, Ionic, Corinthian and Composite.

To the south of the Old Bodleian is the **Radcliffe Camera**, arguably Oxford's best known feature. It was built with money bequeathed by Dr John Radcliffe, a society physician (and physician to William III), and though the rotunda idea was Nicholas Hawksmoor's, the architect was James Gibb who completed it in 1749. 'Camera' is medieval for 'room', the building being Britain's first reading room (in the modern sense of the word). With its classical colonnade and domed roof, it is a resounding success as a piece of architecture, and completed the assembly of buildings at the University's heart. The Camera, which is not open to the public, is now part of the Bodleian Library to which it is linked (and to the New Bodleian - built when the Old library could no longer accommodate all the books - in Broad Street) by an underground passage.

To the south of Radcliffe Camera is **St Mary the Virgin's**

Church, its main entrance on High Street, but accessible from the Camera side. St Mary's is the parish church of Oxford and also the University's Church. It was here that degree and other cere-monies were held until the Sheldonian Theatre was built. The church is in Perpendicular style with little to suggest an earlier building. Externally, the best features are the south porch (in High Street) and the tower/spire. The porch was built in 1637 in Baroque style, with flamboyant twisted columns. The statue of the Virgin in the niche above the doorway caused such outrage among

Radcliffe Camera from St Mary's Church Tower

Lincoln College from St Mary's Church Tower

the Puritans that the head was shot off by a soldier. It was replaced when more restrained times returned. The tower and spire are marvellously elegant, and balance the more classical buildings to the north. Visitors can climb to the tower for a panoramic view of the city. Inside, the most interesting item is the cutaway section at the foot of the last nave column to the north (opposite the pulpit). In 1556 Thomas Cranmer, Archbishop of Canterbury, who had been condemned after his trial with Latimer and Ridley in 1555, returned to Oxford. Latimer and Ridley had already been burned in 1555, but Cranmer had been given leave to appeal. While in prison he had recanted and then retracted several times, but was brought to the church where, it was believed, he would finally recant his Protestantism. A platform was built around the column to raise him above the crowd., but Cranmer failed to recant, instead renouncing his previous recants. He was immediately dragged to Broad Street and burned. Later, the church witnessed the preachings of John Keble and John Newman, leaders of the Oxford Movement which sought to re-introduce Catholic ceremony into the Anglican church. Newman, a vicar of St Mary's, eventually left the Church of England and became a Cardinal.

All Souls College stands to the east of Radcliffe Camera. To the west is **Brasenose College**, founded in 1509 by William Smith, Bishop of Lincoln, and Sir Richard Sutton, a lawyer. The curious name is reputedly from a brass knocker (a 'brazen nose') on the building's first door. The knocker is now claimed to hang behind the high table in the dining hall: it is said to have been stolen by students in the 1330s and to have found its way to Brasenose House in Stamford from where the college retrieved it in 1890. A replacement knocker can be seen on the main gate, and the original (if so it be) can also be viewed. The entrance opposite the Camera leads to the Old Quad, which dates from the founding. The painted sundial on the northern side dates from 1719: from it there is a superb view of Radcliffe Camera and the spire of St Mary's.

Go along Brasenose Lane, beside the college, to reach Turl Street. A short distance to the right from here is the entrance to **Exeter College**. The college was founded in 1314 by the Bishop of Exeter, but nothing remains of the original buildings. The first quad is dominated by the mid-19th century chapel of Sir George Gilbert Scott, its design based on Sainte Chapelle in Paris. Inside there is some good stained glass and a tapestry of the Adoration of the Magi, designed by Edward Burne-Jones and made by William Morris' company. Both the pre-Raphaelites were Exeter men. Other former students were Sir Roger Bannister and J.R.R. Tolkien, author of *The Lord of the Rings*. It is said that Tolkien loved to spend time in the Fellows Garden, a lovely place with a fine view of Radcliffe Square.

Opposite Exeter is **Jesus College**, founded in 1571 by Elizabeth I, but using money provided by Dr Hugh Price, Treasurer of St David's Cathedral. This Welsh ancestry has been maintained, Jesus occasionally being called the Welsh college because of its links with the principality. The chapel has a bust to a non-Welsh student, T.E. Lawrence (of Arabia), though he spent only one term here and, legend has it, mostly occupied himself in studying military architecture in a shed in his parents' garden in north Oxford.

A left turn along Turl Street brings the visitor to **Lincoln Col-**

The Covered Market

lege, founded by Richard Fleming, Bishop of Lincoln, in 1427. It is a small college, but, as Pevsner notes has 'preserved more of the character of a 15th century college than any other in Oxford'. The Front Quad is still as built, having avoided the remodelling of other quads largely because Fleming died in 1431 leaving his college with no funds with which to spoil the original. When the college did expand, it built the Chapel Quad in the 17th century, again leaving Front Quad untouched. The chapel for which the quad is named is in fine Perpendicular style and has some excellent stained glass. Experts are divided on the artist, some seeing the work of Abraham von Linge, while others (including Pevsner) see that of his brother, Bernard. Fleming's intention when founding the college was to train priests in orthodox thinking as the early 15th century was a time of perceived heresy. It is ironical that three centuries later John Wesley was made a Fellow and began his Holy Club, the members of which were to become known as Methodists because of the methodical nature of their devotions. Wesley's old room in the college can be visited.

From the junction of Brasenose Lane and Turl Street go straight ahead, along Market Street, to reach the entrance to the covered market, built in 1774 as a permanent home for the stall holders who were, at that time, spread throughout the city. For sights, sounds and smells the market – almost exclusively a food market – is hard to beat. There is an exit from the market into High Street: turn right to return to Carfax.

Walk 3: St Giles' and the North-West

From Carfax head northwards along Cornmarket Street (*see* Walk 4) to reach Broad Street, on the right. A short detour follows this aptly named street, once the scene of a horse fair, soon reaching the **Oxford Story** on the right. This museum – a well-known Oxford institution because of its prominently displayed emblem of a cycling don – explores the history of the university. The museum, created by the designers of the award-winning Jorvik Centre in York, uses the latest technology – visitors sit at motorized desks for the 'tour' – to bring alive the sights, smells and characters of eight centuries of academic life.

Opposite the museum is **Balliol College**, founded in 1263 by John Balliol of County Durham as an act of penance for insulting the Bishop of Durham. The college was founded to allow sixteen poor scholars to study at Oxford and for much of its life remained a poor relation, but in Victorian times it became very rich as coal was discovered on land, donated by Balliol, in Northumberland. The cash was used to almost completely rebuild the college, little now remaining of earlier buildings. The entrance is into Front Quad whose western and north-western parts are 15th century. The rest is Victorian, as is the larger Garden Quad. The whole college is well laid-out, but somewhat uninspiring: William Morris, the pre-Raphaelite artist, is said to have been moved to create the Society for the Protection of Ancient Buildings by the demolition of Balliol's medieval buildings, and is likely to have been even more dismayed by the replacements. It is sad, because the master at the time, Benjamin Jowett, employed excel-

Martyrs' Monument

lent architects. Jowett may
have been responsible for
destroying a part of history,
but he was the saviour of Balliol, not only using the unex-
pected mining funds to rebuild
and expand the college, but
altering its ethos. From his
time (he was Master from
1870 until 1893) Balliol
became one of the intellectual
centres of the University, producing a stream of eminent
men, including several Prime
Ministers. Matthew Arnold,
whose 'dreaming spires' are
the city's verbal emblem, was
also a Balliol student.

St John's College Garden

Next to Balliol is **Trinity College**, originally founded as
Durham College in 1286 by Durham Cathedral, but refounded in
1555 after the Dissolution of the monasteries. The college is curious in having a simple gated entrance rather than an ornate tower
gateway. The cottages to the side are 17th century, but were pre-
cisely rebuilt in 1969. Beyond the Front Quad is Durham Quad,
in part 14th century. The college's Baroque chapel is thought by
many to be the finest in Oxford: Pevsner goes as far as saying it
is one of the most perfect of its age in Britain. Inside is a carved
reredos which many experts believe to be the work of Grinling
Gibbons, though there is no direct evidence to support this.
Beyond Durham Quad is Garden Quad, originally designed by Sir
Christopher Wren as a single building (the northern side, but now
modified out of recognition). From the quad a gate leads to the
college gardens, a huge and much-loved space. Legend has it that
the delights of picnics and croquet here are the reason for Trinity's comparatively limited success in producing eminent ex-stu-
dents. The college would, of course, dispute both aspects of this

133

suggestion. Beside Trinity is **Blackwells**, the famous bookshop. Begun as a small shop in 1879 by Benjamin Blackwell, it is now the largest and most famous University bookshop, with several miles of shelving.

Back at the junction, our walk continues along Magdalen Street to the **Martyrs' Monument**, erected in the 1840s to the memory of Bishops Latimer and Ridley, and Archbishop Cranmer. The three were burnt at the stake in Broad Street, a cross in the road opposite Balliol College marking the exact spot. To the left, just beyond the Monument, is Beaumont Street. On its near corner is the Randolph Hotel, while opposite is the Taylor Institute for modern language teaching and, beside it, the **Ashmolean Museum**. In the second half of the 17th century John Tradescant, a royal gardener, began a collection of curios, many given to him by sea captains returning with specimens of plants from around the world. His son, also John, continued the collection with some of his own curios from North America. The collection was housed in a Lambeth inn called The Ark, and bequeathed to the Tradescants' friend Elias Ashmole who gave it and his own collection of

The University Museum

antiquities, chiefly coins, to Oxford. The building which now houses the museum was built in 1841 when the museum based on Ashmole's bequest had outgrown its original home. It is now one of the world's great museums. The original Tradescant collection has some extraordinary pieces: Guy Fawkes' lantern, Henry VIII's stirrups and the cloak of Pocohontas' father, while the Greek and Roman antiquity collection of Sir Flinders Petrie, the famous archaeologist, is quite superb. There is also an excellent collec-

St Giles'

tion of Saxon objects, including Alfred's Jewel, claimed to be the finest Saxon artwork discovered to date. Found in Somerset in 1693, the enamel and gold framed piece is named for its inscription – *Aelfred mec heht gewyrcan*, 'Alfred had me made'. It is not, however, a jewel in the accepted sense, being not a brooch, but the head of a pointer used to follow the text in a manuscript. The museum also has superb collections of eastern art and coins, and a collection of western art which includes drawings by Renaissance artists and *The Hunt in the Forest*, a painting by Paolo Uccello.

Continue along St Giles', the scene in September of a two-day fair with medieval origins, soon reaching the entrance to **St John's College** on the right. St John's was first founded (as St Bernard's College) in 1437 for Cistercian monks, but was refounded after the Dissolution by Sir Thomas White, a member of the Guild of Merchant Taylors. St John's is reputedly not only the richest of Oxford's colleges, but one of the richest establishments in Britain. Front Quad, reached from St Giles', is 15th/16th century and includes details from the first founding. The chapel includes the fan-vaulted Baylie Chapel, named for Richard Baylie who lies buried there. Baylie was head of St John's at the time of the Civil War: he was a staunch Royalist, declined to resign (or leave) when Parliament won and was physically ejected from the college. He regained his position at the Restoration.

The most impressive part of the college was built by Baylie's predecessor, Archbishop Laud. This, the Canterbury Quad, is reached by a fan-vaulted passage from Front Quad. It is superb, one of the highlights of the Oxford colleges. The east and west ranges, with their Tuscan arcading, are mirror images, apart from the niche statues, which are of Charles I and Henrietta Maria, his queen. The royal couple were invited to the opening of the Quad, the festivities that accompanied their visit reputedly costing more than the buildings. Canterbury's southern side – now the college library – pre-dates the remainder by a few years and is built around an even earlier section, but in no way diminishes the overall effect. From Front Quad another, later, quad – North Quad – with some very modern buildings is reached. From Canterbury the college gardens – naturalistic and planted with wild flowers, and quite magnificent – are reached, these offering another view of the modern sections of North Quad.

Continue along St Giles', passing **St Cross College**, founded as recently as 1965. In the next street on the left (Pusey Street) is **Regents Park College**, re-sited here from London in 1957. Almost opposite Pusey Street, a detour along Lamb and Play Passage, beside the inn of the same name, leads to Museum Road and the **University Museum**, famous as the venue for the debate between Samuel Wilberforce, the Bishop of Oxford, and Prof Thomas Huxley on Darwin's evolutionary theory. Built in Gothic style in the 1860s, the museum was controversial in its day as the use of the style had previously been confined to churches. The museum houses an extensive collection of natural history specimens including dinosaur skeletons – more than one writer has commentated on the similarity of these skeletons and the structure of the roof – and a famous painting of a live dodo brought to England in 1638.

From the museum a corridor leads to the **Pitt-Rivers Museum of Ethnology**, built in 1885 to house the collection of Lt-Gen. Augustus Henry Lane Fox Pitt-Rivers. Originally a massive collection of over ten thousand items, it has now expanded to almost a million and explores the culture and life-styles of native peoples from Asia, Africa and the Americas. An annex to the museum (well to the north, along the Banbury Road (the A465) houses collections on hunting societies and of musical instruments from all over the world.

Turning left along Parks Road from Museum Road soon reaches **Keble College**, founded in 1868 as a memorial to John Keble, a founder of the Oxford Movement, and raised by public subscription. It was a controversial building in its day, and still raises comment now, its use of multi-coloured brick being a radical departure from the traditional stone. Pevsner is unequivocal in his view: the college is 'actively ugly', a view he expressed before some of the glass and steel additions were completed. But it has its sympathisers – not least its students – and brings many this far just to see what the fuss is about. They also come, more justifiably, to see Holman Hunt's *The Light of the World* in the college chapel.

Back in St Giles', continue north, passing the Eagle and Child Inn, on the corner of Wellington Place – famous as the meeting place of a literary group, including C.S. Lewis and J.R.R. Tolkien, called the Inklings which met there between 1939 and the early 1960s – and **St Benet's Hall**, founded in 1897, then taking the left branch (Woodstock Road) at the fork. Our route now turns left into Little Clarendon Street, but continue along Woodstock Road for a short distance, passing the late 19th century Catholic church of St Aloysius to reach the entrance to **Somerville College**, founded for women students in 1879, but becoming a full college only in 1959. Former students include Indira Gandhi and Margaret Thatcher. Further along Woodstock Road is **Green College**, founded in 1979, but including the Radcliffe Observatory (built in 1794) within its boundaries. Sadly the Observatory cannot be visited. Further again are **St Anne's College**, founded for women in 1879, and **St Anthony's College**, founded in 1948.

Go along Little Clarendon Street and turn left along Walton Street. To the right is **Ruskin College**, named for John Ruskin and not an official college of the University. It was built to educate the working-class folk of 'Jericho', as the poor north-western edge of old Oxford was known. Jericho was called 'Beersheba' – a slum whose inhabitants battled against cholera – by Thomas Hardy in *Jude the Obscure*.

Opposite Beaumont Street, to the left, is the entrance to **Worcester College**, founded in 1714, though there has been a college on the site since 1283. The name derives from Sir Thomas Cookes, a Worcestershire landowner, who re-established the college after the Dissolution had closed the earliest hall. Some 15th century buildings survive, but most date from the 18th century, built to a design by Nicholas Hawksmoor. The college does not have a completely enclosed quad, the open side looking out towards a lake. On the left (southern) edge of the quad are the medieval buildings of Gloucester Hall, the earliest foundation. At the end of this range, a narrow passage leads to the college gardens. It is believed that this passage was the inspiration for the tunnel 'not much larger than a rathole' which led 'to the loveliest garden you ever saw' in *Alice in Wonderland*, as Dodgson and Alice Liddell are known to have explored the Worcester gardens. The gardens are enhanced by a lake, on the far side of which is the Oxford Canal (built in 1790 to link the city with the Grand Union Canal at Napton). A walk around the lake is worthwhile: the naturalistic gardens are a splendid foreground to views of the college, and the lake itself, with its fringe of willows is beautiful. The lake is not natural, having been dug when the gardens were laid out as a 'romantic' park. At the northern end is the Sainsbury Building, Worcester's newest block: it is widely regarded as the most successful piece of modern architecture in the University.

Continue along Worcester Street (the continuation of Walton Street), soon turning left into Gloucester Green, a new pedestrianized square. The city's Tourist Information Office is to the left, with the bus and coach station to the right. An archway leads to the main square where there are several cafés and restaurants. Bear right past the cinema to reach George Street. To the right, in the Old Fire Station, **Curioxity** is an interactive science exhibition which will delight both children and adults. Turn left to return to the junction reached early in the walk, with Broad Street ahead, and turn right along Cornmarket Street to regain Carfax.

Walk 4: The South-West to the Thames

From Carfax go along Cornmarket Street. Soon, to the right, on the far corner of Ship Street, is **St Michael's Church** with a Saxon tower dating from the early 11th century. The tower can be climbed, passing a small exhibition of sacred art, for a good view of central Oxford. Opposite is a lovely medieval building, once the Ship Inn. To the left, opposite Ship Street, is St Michael's Street. Along here, on the left, is the building of the **Oxford Union**, home of the University's famous debating society. It is not open to the public. At the end of St Michael's Street, turn left along New Inn Hall Street, soon passing **St Peter's College**, to the right. The college was founded in 1928, but only became a full University college in 1961. Continue to the road end at Bonn Square (named for Oxford's German 'twin' city).

A short detour now goes right, along New Road, to **Nuffield College**. The college (on the right as you follow New Road) was founded in 1937 by Lord Nuffield – the car magnate, William Morris – and is in Cotswold style, apart from the austere but striking Harkness Tower. Opposite the college the green mound is all that remains of **Oxford Castle**. Continuing to the end of the road, a left turn, then left again along Tidmarsh Lane

Queen Street

leads to St Tomas Street beyond the bridge. Here, to the left, is **Morrells Brewery**, where guided tours explore the art of brewing and include a visit to the Brewers Gate pub where Morrells special brews can be sampled. Returning along New Street, gaunt Oxford Prison is to the right.

From Bonn Square go along St Ebbe's Street (opposite New Inn Hall Street), soon reaching Pembroke Street on the left. Just along the street is the **Museum of Modern Art**. The museum is housed in an old brewery warehouse and is rightly acclaimed for its frequent exhibitions by contemporary international artists in all media. The museum's café – MOMA – is a good place for a coffee during a tour of the city.

Continue along St Ebbe's Street, soon passing **St Ebbe's Church**, built in the 12th century, but rebuilt in the early 19th so that only a doorway of the original remains. The church is named for a 7th century Northumbrian abbess.

Go past Beef Lane, on the left, then turn left along Brewer Street to reach the entrance to **Pembroke College**, founded in 1624 and named for the University's then Chancellor, the Earl of Pembroke. Chapel Quad is largely 19th century, but looks much

Faculty of Music from Broad Walk

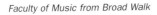

St Aldate's

older. The statue of James I in the tower niche is a reminder that he was the nominal founder (though the money came from elsewhere). The chapel for which the quad is named has excellent stained glass and a fine painted ceiling, each in Renaissance style. Opposite Pembroke is **Campion Hall**, founded by the Jesuits in 1895.

Continue along Brewer Street to reach St Aldate's, with Christ Church to the left. Turn right, soon reaching **Alice's Shop**, the original of the 'Sheep Shop' drawn by Tenniel for *Through the Looking Glass*. In real life, Alice Liddell bought barley sugar here: in fantasy Alice was served by a grumpy sheep. The shop sells Alice in Wonderland souvenirs.

Further on, to the left is the University's Faculty of Music which houses the **Bate Collection of Musical Instruments**. The collection, started with a donation to the University by Philip Bate in 1963, is one of the best of its kind in Britain, exploring the development of European instruments, and also including some from other parts of the world. The collection includes the harpsichord played by Haydn when he visited Oxford in 1791 to receive an honorary degree.

Continue along St Aldate's to reach **Folly Bridge** over the

River Thames, or Isis as the river within the city is known. This is believed by many historians to have been the site of the 'Oxen Ford' which named the city. As at Magdalen Bridge, punts can be hired here. The traditional punt is about 8m (25ft) long and carries four passengers as well as the punter, who propels the boat with a 5m (16ft) pole. It looks easy, but...

From the bridge, a walk along the river past the Head of the River Inn soon reaches the **College Boat Houses**. It is on this section of the river that Eights Week is held during the summer term. The races, between college eights, are settled by bumping – catching the boat in front. The winning college is Head of the River. The better known race against Cambridge is, of course, raced on the Thames between Putney and Mortlake in London.

From Folly Bridge, follow St Aldate's back to Carfax.

Outlying Colleges

Visitors determined to see all forty-one Oxford Colleges will need to travel further out from the city centre. Behind Wadham College, in Mansfield Road, are **Manchester College**, founded in Manchester as a theological college in 1786 and transferred to Oxford in 1889, and **Mansfield College**, founded in Birmingham in 1838, also as a theological college, and transferred to Oxford in 1886. To the north-east of Mansfield, **Linacre College** became a college only in 1965.

Reached from the Banbury Road are **Lady Margaret Hall**, founded for women students in 1878 and **Wolfson College**, founded in 1965 as Iffley College but renamed after a substantial donation by Lord Wolfson. **St Hugh's College**, reached from the Woodstock Road, was founded in 1886 for women students, becoming a full college in 1959.

To the east of the city is **St Catherine's College**, founded in 1963. The college buildings, in uncompromising yellow brick, received the enthusiastic support of Pevsner, but also have their detractors. The college stands in delightful grounds.

Finally, to the south of the city in Kennington lies **Templeton College**, which is not open to the public.

ADDRESSES AND OPENING TIMES

CARFAX TOWER
(01865 792653)
❖
OPEN: Apr–Oct, daily 10am–5.30pm; Nov–Mar, daily
10am–3.30pm (closed from 25 Dec–1 Jan)

MUSEUM OF OXFORD,
Blue Boar Lane (01865 815559)
❖
OPEN: all year, Tues–Sat 10am–5pm

CHRIST CHURCH PICTURE GALLERY,
Oriel Square (01865 276172)
❖
OPEN: all year, Mon–Sat 10.30am–1pm and 2–5.30pm, Sun
2–5.30pm; closes 4.30pm Oct–Easter

BOTANIC GARDENS,
High Street (01865 276920)
❖
OPEN: all year, daily 9am–5pm (4.30pm Oct–Easter);
glasshouses open daily 10am–4pm (2–4pm Oct–Easter);
closed Good Friday and Christmas Day

SHELDONIAN THEATRE,
Broad Street (01865 277299)
❖
OPEN: all year, Mon–Sat 10am–12.30pm and 2–4.30pm,
but sometimes closed for concert rehearsals

MUSEUM OF THE HISTORY OF SCIENCE,
Broad Street (01865 277820)
❖
OPEN: all year, Tues–Sat 12noon–4pm
closed at Easter and Christmas

BODLEIAN LIBRARY,
Old School Quad (01865 277165)
❖
OPEN: all year, Mon–Fri 9am–5pm, Sat 9am–12.30pm; guided tours of the Divinity School and Duke Humfrey's Library on same days at 10.30am, 11.30am, 2pm and 3pm (not Sat afternoon)

ST MARY THE VIRGIN CHURCH TOWER
❖
OPEN: all year, Mon–Sat 9am–7pm (5pm from Oct–March), Sun 12noon–5.30pm (dusk from Oct–March)

OXFORD STORY,
6 Broad Street (01865 790055)
❖
OPEN: April–Oct, daily 9.30am–5pm (closes at 6pm in July and August); Nov–March, daily 10am–4.30pm (5pm on Sat and Sun)

ASHMOLEAN MUSEUM,
Beaumont Street (01865 278000)
❖
OPEN: all year, Tues–Sat 10am–4pm, Sun 2–4pm; open Bank Holiday Mon 2–5pm, but closed for several days at Christmas, on 1 Jan and Good Friday–Easter Monday

UNIVERSITY MUSEUM,
Parks Road (01865 272950)
❖
OPEN: all year, Mon–Sat 12noon–5pm

PITT-RIVERS MUSEUM OF ETHNOLOGY,
Parks Road (entrance through University Museum) (01865 270928)
❖
OPEN: all year, Mon–Sat 12noon–5pm

PITT-RIVERS MUSEUM ANNEXE,
60 Banbury Road (01865 270949)
❖
OPEN: all year, Mon–Sat 1–4.30pm

CURIOXITY,
40 George Street (01865 794494)
❖
OPEN: all year, Sat, Sun and School holidays (including
half–terms) 10am–4pm

ST MICHAEL'S TOWER,
Cornmarket Street
❖
OPEN: all year, daily 10am–5pm (4pm from Nov–March)

MORRELLS BREWERY,
St Thomas Street (01865 813036)
❖
OPEN: June–Sept, daily tours at 12noon; Oct–May, tours on
Sat and Sun at 12noon; closed Christmas Day, Boxing Day,
New Year's Eve and New Year's Day

MUSEUM OF MODERN ART,
30 Pembroke Street (01865 722733)
❖
OPEN: all year, Tues–Sat 10am–6pm (but 9pm on Thurs),
Sun 2–6pm

BATE COLLECTION OF MUSICAL INSTRUMENTS,
Faculty of Music, St Aldate's (01865 276139)
❖
OPEN: all year, Mon–Fri 2–5pm; also open on Sat during
University terms, 10am–12noon

Punting

Boats are available from:
C Howard and Son, Magdalen Bridge (01865 761586)
Salter Brothers Ltd, Folly Bridge (01865 243421)

The Colleges

ALL SOULS COLLEGE,
High Street
❖
OPEN: all year, Mon–Fri 2–4.30pm

BALLIOL COLLEGE,
Broad Street
❖
OPEN: term only, daily 2–5pm

BRASENOSE COLLEGE,
Radcliffe Square
❖
OPEN: all year, daily 10–11.30am and 2–4.30pm

CAMPION HALL,
Brewer Street
❖
Not open to the public

CHRIST CHURCH,
St Aldate's
❖
OPEN: all year, Mon–Sat 9.30am–5.30pm, Sun
11.30am–5.30pm; closed on Christmas Day

CORPUS CHRISTI COLLEGE,
Merton Street

OPEN: all year, daily 1.30–4.30pm

EXETER COLLEGE,
Turl Street

OPEN: all year; term, daily 2–5pm; vacation, daily
10am–5pm

GREEN COLLEGE,
Woodstock Road

OPEN: Enquire at Porter's Lodge

HERTFORD COLLEGE,
Catte Street

OPEN: all year, daily 10am–dusk

JESUS COLLEGE,
Turl Street

OPEN: all year, daily 2–4.30pm

KEBLE COLLEGE,
Parks Road

OPEN: all year, daily 2–5pm

LADY MARGARET HALL,
Norham Gardens

OPEN: gardens only, all year, daily 10am–dusk

LINACRE COLLEGE,
St Cross Road

❖

OPEN: all year, daily 9am–5pm

LINCOLN COLLEGE,
Turl Street

❖

OPEN: all year, Mon–Sat 2–5pm, Sun 11am–5p
(open to small family groups only);
John Wesley's room is open daily 2–5pm

MAGDALEN COLLEGE,
High Street

❖

OPEN: all year, Mon–Fri 12noon–6pm, Sat and Sun 2–6pm

MANCHESTER COLLEGE,
Mansfield Road

❖

OPEN: Chapel only; all year, Mon–Fri 9am–5.30pm

MANSFIELD COLLEGE,
Mansfield Road

❖

OPEN: all year, Mon–Fri 9am–5pm

MERTON COLLEGE,
Merton Street

❖

OPEN: all year, Mon–Fri 2–4pm, Sat and Sun 10am–4pm;
the Beerbohm Collection can be viewed as part of a guided
tour of the library – tours are available (maximum five
people) Mon–Fri 2–4pm

NEW COLLEGE,
New College Lane
❖
OPEN: Easter–Oct, daily 11am–5pm, Nov–Easter, daily
2–4pm

NUFFIELD COLLEGE,
New Road
❖
OPEN: Quad only; Mon–Sat 9am–5pm, Sun 10am–5pm

ORIEL COLLEGE,
Oriel Square
❖
OPEN: all year, daily 2–5pm

PEMBROKE COLLEGE,
Pembroke Square
❖
OPEN: all year, daily 10am–dusk

QUEEN'S COLLEGE,
High Street
❖
OPEN: only if accompanied by an official Oxford Guide

REGENT'S PARK COLLEGE,
Pusey Street
❖
Not open to the public

ST ANNE'S COLLEGE,
Woodstock Road
❖
OPEN: all year except 20 Dec–2 Jan, daily 9am–5pm

ST ANTHONY'S COLLEGE,
Woodstock Road
❖
Not open to the public

ST BENET'S HALL,
St Giles'
❖
Not open to the public

ST CATHERINE'S COLLEGE,
Manor Road
❖
OPEN: gardens only; all year, daily 2–5pm

ST CROSS COLLEGE,
St Giles'
❖
Not open to the public

ST EDMUND HALL,
Queen's Lane
❖
OPEN: all year, daily during daylight hours

ST HILDA'S COLLEGE,
Cowley Place
❖
OPEN: term time only; Mon–Fri 2–5pm

ST HUGH'S COLLEGE,
St Margaret's Road
❖
OPEN: all year, daily 9am–5pm

ST JOHN'S COLLEGE,
St Giles'

❖

OPEN: all year, daily 1–5pm

ST PETER'S COLLEGE,
New Inn Hall Street

❖

OPEN: all year, daily 10am–12noon and 2–6pm

SOMERVILLE COLLEGE,
Woodstock Road

❖

OPEN: all year, daily 2–5.30pm

TEMPLETON COLLEGE,
Kennington

❖

Not open to the public

TRINITY COLLEGE,
Broad Street

❖

OPEN: all year, daily 10.30am–12noon and 2–4pm

UNIVERSITY COLLEGE,
High Street

❖

OPEN: enquire at Porter's Lodge

WADHAM COLLEGE,
Parks Road

❖

OPEN: all year, daily 1–4.30pm

WOLFSON COLLEGE,
Linton Road

❖

OPEN: all year, daily 9am–5pm

....

WORCESTER COLLEGE,
Worcester Street

❖

OPEN: Easter–Oct, Mon–Sat 2–5.45pm; Nov–Easter,
Mon–Sat 2pm–dusk; guided parties
(maximum six people) only

(Opposite) Mapledurham Lock

THE SOUTHERN CHILTERNS

Henley-on-Thames

As Henley derives, in part, from the Saxon word for a meadow, it is likely that there was a settlement of some sort before the Norman Conquest, though there is no mention of it in the Domesday Book. In the medieval period the town became important as it was set at the point on the River Thames which was the limit to trading vessels of a reasonable size. Though boats could, and did, travel further, the river became increasingly difficult to navigate, and timber and farm produce were brought over land to the town for shipment to London. The building of a bridge in the late 12th century guaranteed Henley's prosperity, the town becoming a coach stop *en route* to the capital. The town's history was uneventful, allowing it to prosper in a quiet way into the graceful and elegant riverside town we see today.

A tour of the town should start at the Thames bridge. The present bridge dates from 1786, replacing one damaged in the Civil War – though damaged, it took a hundred years for it to be declared unsafe and thirty more before the replacement was built beside it. As noted above, there is evidence for a bridge as early as the late 12th century, work in 1984 uncovering mason's marks which have been dated to around 1170. Downstream of the bridge the town's famous regatta takes place each year in early July. The rowing races began in 1839 as a single day event, becoming the Royal Regatta in 1851 under the patronage of Prince Albert, but now take place over five days. A new museum explores not only the history of the regatta, but the history of the river with its associated pageantry. It is located in Mill Meadows, beside the Thames on the southern edge of town (follow Thameside from the bridge, then River Terrace and Meadow Road to reach the museum).

From the bridge, walk up Hart Street. This is almost certainly Henley's oldest street and has an array of fine houses, mostly from the 15th/16th centuries, even though some now have 18th century, Georgian, façades. To the right is St Mary's Church, originally built in the early 13th century, but rebuilt on a grander scale in the early 15th. The tower is a century younger, the gift of a Bishop of Lincoln who was born in Henley. Inside there is some excellent Victorian stained glass and the marvellous alabaster and black marble tomb to Lady Elizabeth Periam, who died in 1621, showing her lying on her side supported on her right elbow. Behind the church is the early 15th century Chantry House, a fine timber-framed, overhung building built as a school for poor boys and now the church hall, and a collection of almshouses, originally built in the 17th century, but rebuilt in the 18th.

On the southern (left) side of Hart Street, just before No. 40 (the

Hart Street, Henley-on-Thames

Lady Periam's Tomb, St Mary's Church
Henley-on-Thames

Henley Regatta

Tandoori restaurant) is the Speaker's House where William Lenthall, the Speaker of the Long Parliament and a signatory of Charles I's death warrant, is said to have been born in 1591. In 1642 when the King arrived at the House of Commons, demanding the arrest of five MPs, he ordered Lenthall to identify them: the Speaker famously responded that he had 'neither eyes to see, nor tongue to speak, but as the House directs me'. Lenthall retired in 1654 and was pardoned for his part in the King's death after the Restoration. He died in 1662. Further on, and across the street, are the Old White Hart and Catherine Wheel inns, which have stood since the 15th century.

At the cross-roads Duke Street is to the left. There are some 17th century houses here and in Friday Street (first left from Duke Street) there are some equally good 18th century buildings. Ahead is Market Place, lined with good, mainly 18th century, houses. At the top is the Town Hall, built in 1901 in grand style. It has maintained its function, but now also houses the Tourist Information Centre.

Turn right along Bell Street, in which there are some superb timber-framed houses, some dating from the 16th century. The Olde Bell Inn was renamed in 1920: previously it had been the Duke of Cumberland, taking that name after the Duke's victory at Culloden had ended the Jacobite threat.

Now turn right along New Street. On the left corner, Corner House is 15th century, possibly the oldest in the street as most of the other buildings are 18th or 19th century. The marvellous exceptions are Ann Boleyn and Tudor Cottages, which pre-date the name, probably also dating from the 15th century. The name dates from Henry VIII's use of Phyllis Court (beside the river and now a Country Club) as a hunting lodge, members of his Court using the cottages as lodgings. Mary Boleyn, the sister of Anne, also lived locally, having married the owner of Grey's court. The cottages lie beyond the Kenton Theatre which claims to be the fourth oldest in England, having been built in 1805, though it has not been used continuously as a theatre, spending much of its time as chapel and school. It became a theatre again in 1951.

Follow New Street into Riverside, rejoining the bridge beyond the Red Lion Inn. It was here that the 18th century poet William Shenstone penned the often quoted:

> Whoe'er has travell'd life's dull round,
> Where'er his stages may have been,
> May sigh to think he still has found
> The warmest welcome, at an inn.

The river at Henley-on-Thames

TOUR 5: North from the Thames

In this first short tour from Henley we explore the south-western tip of the Chilterns, journeying between the Thames and the A4130.

To the west of Henley the AONB follows the wooded edge of the Chilterns, using minor roads as its borders and so cutting an angular path through the country. The shortest route to the Thames at Mapledurham, where the AONB re-establishes itself on the northern bank, is along minor roads through Sonning Common, perhaps going through **Harpsden** where three 19th century barns have gable walls made of wooden wallpaper printing blocks. At **Sonning Common**, the Herb Farm has a wide range of herbs, old roses, cottage garden plants and wildflowers for sale, as well as oils, sauces, toiletries and so on, made from herbs. There is also a hedge maze, based on an 8th century Saxon manuscript, with over $1\frac{1}{2}$km (1 mile) of paths. The quickest way to the Thames – unless you are following the commuters – is to follow the A4155 towards Reading's northern suburbs and the A4074 away from them.

Reading appears at first glance to be just another of the suburb-towns of London rather than a likely tourist destination. However, it has a rich history and a visit to the heart of the old town is rewarding. Make your way to the Tourist Information Centre in the Town Hall in Blagrave Street, just a short step from the main railway station. In the same building is the town museum, which explores the town's occasionally colourful history. It houses the only full-scale replica of the Bayeux Tapestry (stitched in Leek, Staffordshire in 1885). The Norman Conquest was the most significant event in the town's history, for although it was a Saxon settlement, it was the founding of Reading Abbey by Henry I in 1121 that began its rise in prosperity. Henry was buried in the abbey after his death in 1136.

Reading Abbey occupied a 35-acre site and it is that area which is of most interest to visitors. The Town Hall/museum lies at one edge of the monastic site, where the guests' dormitory once stood.

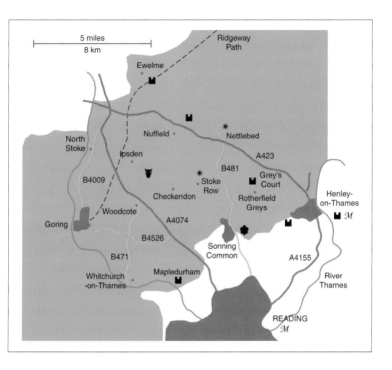

Close by is St Laurence's Church, built as part of the abbey complex and the most beautiful of the town's churches. It has some fine memorial brasses. The churchyard was the site of the execution of Hugh Faringdon, the Abbot of Reading Abbey. In 1539 he refused to recognize Henry VIII as head of the church and was hanged, drawn and quartered.

Behind the Town Hall, Forbury Gardens is a haven of peace in the bustling town centre: in it stands what little remains of the abbey's buildings and a memorial to Henry I. There is also the Maiwand Lion, a memorial to the men of the Berkshire Regiment killed at Maiwand during the Afghan campaign. The lion was erected in 1886 and, at 10m (33ft) long and 5m (16ft) high, was the biggest standing lion in the world. The lion weighs 16 tons.

Mapledurham Mill

Forbury Gardens,
Reading

Beyond the abbey ruins, where once stood the monastic infirmary and gardens, is Reading Prison, a gaunt Victorian building made world-famous by the *Ballad of Reading Gaol*, the poem written by its most famous inmate, Oscar Wilde. After the trial which scandalized Victorian Britain, Wilde was imprisoned here from 1895–97. From Chestnut Walk, which follows the prison wall, a towpath beside an arm of the River Kennet leads to Blake's Lock Museum, housed in the old pumping station of Blake's Weir. Here the 19th and early 20th century history of Reading is explored with reconstructions of a bakery, printers and men's hairdresser, and exhibits on local industries and the canal. There is also one of the most ornate gypsy caravans still in existence, a masterpiece from 1910. Further away, about 3km (2 miles) from the town centre along the A327, the Museum of English Rural Life at Reading University's Whiteknights site explores the last 200 years of farming practices and country crafts.

Back in the AONB, **Mapledurham** is a hamlet dominated by a manor house which is the centrepiece of a visit back in time to the

England when the local squire ruled a scattering of houses, a church and a mill. The house dates from Elizabeth I's reign and is the E-plan of the period. It is a large, beautifully symmetric house set off by large lawns. Inside there is an elegant oak staircase and some original plasterwork. There are also good collections of furniture and paintings. The old stables house a tea room and gift shop. Beside the house is the church. The first church here preceded the house, but was comprehensively restored in 1863, the tower being refaced in flint and brick, and topped by a tiled pyramid. Inside there are some excellent memorials, the best being that to Sir Robert Bardolf who died in 1395. The brass is 1.78m (almost 6ft) long and quite superb. Look, too, for the tomb chest of Sir Richard and Lady Blount, for whom the house was built, on which the pair lie in effigy. The church is also unusual in having a section railed off from the main body: this is the Bardolph chapel which remains the private property of the house's Roman Catholic owners. St Margaret's, Mapledurham is one of Britain's few Protestant churches to have a Catholic enclave.

Beyond the church is the hamlet's watermill. There has been a mill on the site since Saxon times, the present one dating from the 15th century. It is the only surviving mill on the Thames and flour ground on site can be bought. The village is completed by a row of early 17th century almshouses.

Swan Upping

Mapledurham Lock is also one of the best places to watch the annual **Swan-Upping** on the Thames. Swans were once a royal table bird – but not, it is said, one which would appeal to today's palate – and were protected in the same way as deer. Certain guilds were also allowed to take birds and a series of nicks for the birds' bills were invented to dissuade or capture poachers. All un-nicked birds belonged to the crown. Today two of the original guilds, the Dyers' and Vintners' Companies, make an annual trip along the Thames from Sunbury to Abingdon to capture the year's cygnets and nick the bills according to the ownership of the parent birds. The 'upping' involves boats with flags, men in uniforms, a capture procedure which is often a failure and invariably hilarious (and occasionally on the edge of giving the capturer a soaking), and a good lunch which usually means that the afternoon's events are even less well co-ordinated. Swan-upping can be viewed from anywhere along the route, but is usually best seen from locks or the day's start/finish points. Within the AONB, that means Marlow where Day 2 ends and Day 3 starts, Mapledurham or Goring Locks on Day 4, and Moulsford where Day 4 ends and Day 5 starts.

Maharajah's Well, Stoke Row

To continue the tour, follow minor roads to **Woodcote**. Here, and at **Whitchurch-on-Thames** to the south, the churches are mid-19th century, but built in late Norman style. In this area the magnificent Chilterns woodlands are first seen. At **Goring Heath**, between Mapledurham and Woodcote, a superb walk heads for the

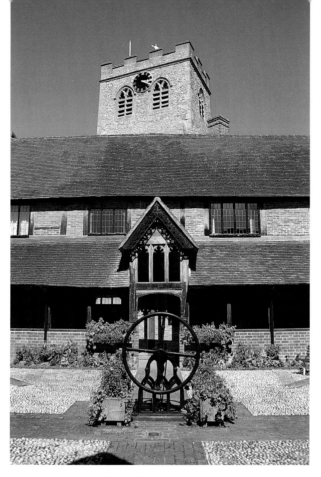

The Almshouses and Church, Ewelme

woods to the east of the cross-roads. Nearby, the 18th century almshouses of Alnut's Hospital are visible from the road.

From the main road (the A4074) near Woodcote, a minor road leads to Checkendon and Stoke Row. The neat Norman flint church at **Checkendon** has a memorial window to Eric Kennington, the friend of T.E. Lawrence, by Lawrence Whistler. Nearby **Stoke Row** is famous for the Maharajah's Well, the gift of Maharajah of Benares to E.A. Reade for his assistance with a water project in Benares. The well is over 110m (365ft) deep and capped with a machinery structure which is itself topped by a gold dome. There is fine woodland to the east of both villages, and a superb walk of about 13km (8 miles) links the two with **Ipsden** through woodland to the west, passing Braziers Park, a fine late 17th century house built, in part, by prisoners from Oxford Gaol as the warden was a part-time architect and builder. Close to Ipsden is Wellplace Zoo which has a collection of small mammals and birds, a pets' corner and a museum with exhibits on dinosaurs. There is also a children's play area and a coffee shop.

From Ipsden, rejoin the A4074 and turn right, heading north to the roundabout outside Wallingford. The Ridgeway National Trail reaches this roundabout, too, having followed the Thames northwards from Goring through **North Stoke** where the church has two medieval wall paintings, rare survivals of the Puritan purges. The Trail heads east from the roundabout, following Grim's Ditch to reach Nuffield, where we shall see it again. But we head northeast, taking the minor road to **Ewelme**, one of the most interesting villages in this part of the AONB. At the village centre is a group of late 15th century buildings, the gift of Alice, Duchess of Suffolk, the grand-daughter of Geoffrey Chaucer. The church was rebuilt in 1432, though the tower is from an earlier building, and has survived virtually intact, avoiding the worst excesses of later restorers. With its square lines and embattlements, it is elegant and impressive, though perhaps too stocky to be beautiful. Inside there is a fine font, dating from 1475, and the magnificent tomb of Duchess Alice on which she lies in alabaster effigy. The splendour of the carving and Alice's coronet is sharply contrasted by the shrivelled cadaver beneath. The contrast is no accident: this is a *memento mori*, a lesson that both rich and poor end this way and should lead their lives accordingly. There are other fine memorials too, including a brass and tomb for Alice's parents. The 15th century stained glass is also extremely interesting.

Below the church are a group of almshouses, founded in 1437 to house thirteen men. The almshouses are in brick, one of the first uses of brick in the county, and are built around a quadrangle, reflecting the style of the Oxford colleges. The village school was

The Old Kiln, Nettlebed

also founded in 1437 and is the oldest in Europe to have been in continuous use since its foundation. Originally there was one more building, the palace that was home to the Duke and Duchess. Legend has it that Chaucer visited the palace as a guest of his grand-daughter, but the date of his death and her marriage seem to conflict with this story. Another legend has Henry VIII spending a honeymoon at the palace, though which honeymoon is open to question. The most likely seems to be that with Catherine Howard, though there is a tradition that it was Anne Boleyn and that she pushed the King into village pond during one playful moment. Much later it was at Ewelme that Jerome K. Jerome, author of *Three Men in a Boat*, spent the last years of his life, in a farmhouse to the south-east of the village centre. He is buried in the churchyard, his headstone answering the question many ask: what did the 'K.' stand for. It was Klapka.

From Ewelme, follow minor roads south to the A423 and turn left for Henley-on-Thames, soon reaching **Nuffield**. For thirty years until his death in 1963 the village was the home of William Morris, Lord Nuffield the motor car pioneer whose career we touched upon in Oxford. His home, Nuffield Place – to the left of the main road, the other side from the village, as you approach – was built in 1914, but is most notable for the furnishings, which are largely as they were in the 1930s when the house was first occupied by Lord and Lady Nuffield. Though some furniture is antique, much was custom-made, making the house a virtual museum of 1930s style. The house stands in large gardens laid out just after building was completed and untouched since then. Lord Nuffield is buried in the village churchyard.

Continue along the main road to **Nettlebed**, a brickmaking centre since the 15th century, where one ancient kiln can still be seen.

The kiln is in a road unimaginatively (but accurately) called The Old Kiln just off the road, to the left, for Crocker End. To the north of Nettlebed, and to both sides of the main road beyond, there is superb woodland, offering fine walking.

Continue through the woodland to Bix, from where a minor road turns right though the delightful Lambridge Wood to reach **Grey's Court**. The oldest part of this extremely picturesque house is the tower which dates from 1347 when Sir John de Grey was granted a 'licence to crenellate', building a fortified manor (or altering an existing one, as the de Greys had held the site since the Conquest). Of the rest of Sir John's house little remains, as it was rebuilt and enlarged several times through to the 18th century (though the de Greys were no longer the owners, the last of their line being killed at the Battle of Bosworth). The major rebuild of Sir John's house was by Sir Francis Knollys, Treasurer to Elizabeth I and one-time guardian of Mary, Queen of Scots (though not at Grey's Court). Knollys was husband of a niece of Anne Boleyn, and therefore cousin of the Queen, that doubtless being a help in his career. His rebuild is the reason for the Tudor

The Archbishop's Maze, Grey's Court

look to parts of the building, and for the Tudor Wheelhouse where a donkey hauled water from a deep well. There are also excellent walled gardens, including old rose types and a kitchen garden, and a curious maze.

The church in nearby **Rotherfield Greys** houses several fine monuments to owners of Grey's Court. Robert de Grey, who died in 1387, has a magnificent brass $1\frac{1}{2}$m (almost 5ft) long depicting him in full armour and helmet. Sir Francis and Lady Katherine Knollys have a

The Knollys Memorial, Rotherfield Greys

large tomb, complete with effigies of them and the kneeling figures of their children – unmissable. Interestingly, despite her effigy lying here, Katherine Knollys lies in Westminster Abbey, at the insistence of Elizabeth I.

From Rotherfield Greys, follow minor roads back to Henley-on-Thames.

ADDRESSES AND OPENING TIMES

RIVER AND ROWING MUSEUM,
Mill Meadow, Henley-on-Thames (01491 415600)

OPEN: all year, Mon–Sat 10am–5pm, Sun 11am–5pm.
Closes at 4pm from Nov–March

CHANTRY HOUSE,
Hart Street, Henley-on-Thames (01491 578034)

OPEN: all year, Wed, Thu and Sat 10am–12noon

HERB FARM AND SAXON MAZE,
Peppard Road, Sonning Common (0118 972 4220)

OPEN: Herb Farm March-Nov, Tue–Sun and Bank Holiday
Mon 10am-5pm, Dec, daily until 24th 10am–5pm, Jan and
Feb, Tue–Sun 11am–4pm; Saxon Maze Easter–Oct half
term, Tue–Sun and Bank Holiday Mon 10am–5pm

MUSEUM OF READING,
Town Hall, Blagrave Street (0118 939 9800)

OPEN: all year, Tue–Sat 10am–5pm, Sun and Bank Holidays
2–5pm

BLAKE'S LOCK MUSEUM,
Gasworks Road (off Kenavon Drive),
Reading (0118 939 0918)

OPEN: all year, Tue–Fri 10am–5pm, Sat, Sun
and Bank Holidays 2–5pm

MUSEUM OF ENGLISH RURAL LIFE,
University of Reading, Whiteknights,
Reading (0118 931 8663)

OPEN: all year Tue–Sat 10am–1pm and 2–4.30pm;
closed on Bank Holidays

MAPLEDURHAM HOUSE AND MILL,
Mapledurham (0118 972 3350)

OPEN: Easter–Sept, Sat, Sun and Bank Holiday Mon; house
2.30–5pm, mill 1–4pm

SWAN UPPING

Usually held in third week of July; details of exact dates and
likely times at best observation points can be obtained from
Her Majesty's Swan Marker, Cookham Bridge,
Cookham–on–Thames, Berkshire SL6 9SN (01628 523030)

MAHARAJAH'S WELL,
Stoke Row (01491 681868)

OPEN: all year, daily during daylight hours

WELLPLACE ZOO
Ipsden (01491 680473/680092)

OPEN: Easter–Sept, daily 10am–5pm; Oct–Easter, Sat and
Sun 10am–5pm or dusk

NUFFIELD PLACE
Nuffield (01491 836654)

OPEN: May–Sept on selected Sundays 2–5pm;
ring for details of exact schedule

GREY'S COURT (National Trust)
Rotherfield Greys (01491 628529)

OPEN: house April–Sept, Mon, Wed and Fri 2–6pm, closed
Good Friday; garden all year, daily except Thu and Sun,
2–6pm, closed Good Friday

TOUR 6: Henley-on-Thames and Marlow

In this tour we continue our exploration of the south-western Chilterns, covering the area from the A423 to the M40.

Leave Henley along the A423 towards Wallingford, but at Lower Assendon turn right along the B480 for Watlington. Soon the road is the border between Oxfordshire and Berkshire, but the first village, **Stonor**, is firmly in the former. A left turn in the village leads to Maidensgrove. Beyond the village there is a fine piece of woodland: there is a car park here and a nature trail through a designated Nature Reserve.

Stonor Park, to the north-east of Stonor village, has belonged to the same family since at least the 12th century, and the present house, largely dating from the 16th century, includes sections of a 13th century one. It is beautifully positioned: as Leland, the Elizabethan traveller, noted, it is 'clyminge on an hille', the hill topped by beech woods. The house has some exquisite furnishings and fine art, including tapestries and bronzes as well as paint-

Stonor Park

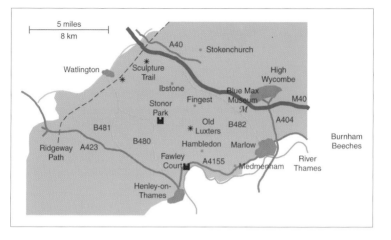

ings. Stonor was a Catholic house even when Catholicism carried the threat of death, and still has a Catholic chapel. In 1581 the first English Jesuit martyr, St Edmund Campion, was given sanctuary here and wrote a book during his stay. Campion was arrested and hanged soon after leaving Stonor. He was canonized in 1970. An exhibition in the house deals with St Edmund's life and times.

A public footpath runs through the deer park which surrounds Stonor House – there is a fine view of the house from it – and this can be used to reach Southend and Turville Heath, a superb walk, returning through Turville Park. But we continue along the B480, passing through several more sections of beautiful woodland and crossing the Ridgeway National Trail, which is now following the Icknield Way, the prehistoric track along the downland scarp. **Watlington**, at the foot of the scarp, is an old market town with a collection of narrow, busy streets. The Market Hall, at the intersection of the three main streets, was built in 1665. Its ground floor was an open-arcaded market area, with the first floor being occupied by the town school. The church, a little way from the Market Hall, has a 15th century tower, but the remainder is from a rebuild in the 1870s. Inside, there are two good 16th century brasses.

171

From Watlington, follow the minor road which heads south-eastwards, climbing back up the steep scarp to regain the wooded Chilterns on Watlington Hill, a National Trust site of almost a hundred acres of downland and woodland. The curious obelisk cut into the chalk dates from 1764. It was cut by Edward Horne, a Watlington man who felt that the town church needed a spire. In the absence of the cash or power to raise one, he had this chalk spire cut so that the church appeared to have a spire when viewed from his house.

Just beyond the car park, on Christmas Common – reputedly named for a Christmas truce between local Civil War troops in 1643 – turn left along the minor road for Kingston Blount and Chinnor to reach the **Chiltern Sculpture Trail**. The trail links a series of outdoor sculptures, some permanent, others temporary, in Cowleaze Wood, a working forest with a mix of deciduous and conifer trees, and, in spring, carpets of bluebells followed by primroses and violets. At the time of writing there are around two dozen sculptures in a variety of media – wood, steel, bronze, even a polypropylene carpet – and the forest trees also form part of some works. To see all the sculptures requires a walk of about 5km (3 miles), but a laid path of about 3km (2 miles) links the majority.

From the Sculpture Trail site, continue along the minor road, crossing the

'Nature Girl'
Chilterns Sculpture Park

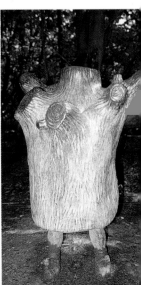

Watlington

M40 motorway to reach the A40. To the left from here is Aston Wood, another beautiful, National Trust-owned section of Chiltern woodland. The Trust land forms part of the Aston Rowant National Nature Reserve, set up to preserve the beech woods and grazed grassland, the latter being home to orchids and gentians. Turn right towards Stokenchurch, crossing the border into Buckinghamshire. Our route turns right on the minor road for Ibstone and Fingest; **Stokenchurch**, ahead, is an old chair-making village, the legs and backs made from Chiltern timber, and cane or rush seating made from willow canes or rushes hauled all the way from the Thames. Hannah Ball, a pioneer of the Sunday School movement, is buried in the churchyard.

Ibstone has a church housing one of the oldest wooden pulpits in England. The church is a little removed from the present village site, legend having it that repeated attempts to build a new church closer to the newer cottages were consistently thwarted by the Devil. Continue along the narrow, but lovely, road towards Fingest, passing below a twelve-sided smock mill, built in the 18th century, but on a site that had been occupied by windmills since the 13th century. The village is proud to note that the mill featured in the film *Chitty Chitty Bang Bang*. The mill is now a private house.

Fingest has one of Buckinghamshire's most famous and most photographed churches. St Bartholomew's has a massive Norman tower 18m (60ft) high and 8m (26ft) square, a structure more often seen in a castle than a parish church. The odd saddleback roof is a much later – 17th or 18th century – addition. The church at nearby **Turville** has a much more conventional tower dating from the 15th century. It is said that during the 19th century an 11-year-old village girl had a fit and fell into a coma from which she did not awaken for ten years, her devoted mother keeping her alive by feeding her liquids with a spoon. Though 21 when she awoke, the girl had no memory of the passage of time and acted as though she were still 11.

To the south of Fingest and Turville – take the minor road for Hambleden and turn right as signed – is Old Luxters, the **Chiltern**

Fingest Church

Valley Winery and Brewery where real ales are brewed and wines bottled. There is also a gallery in a large barn where art exhibitions and concerts are held.

From Fingest take the minor road heading northeast to reach the B482 and turn right along it. Soon a left turn leads to the **Wycombe Air Park**, set close to the M40, and to High Wycombe. Here, the Blue Max Movie Museum has a collection of aircraft made famous by their use in films and television series, including some from the *Battle of Britain* and *Those Magnificent Men in Their Flying Machines*, and, more recently, from *Indiana Jones and the Last Crusade*. Return to the B482 and turn right, descending gently to reach Marlow.

Marlow, as Jerome K. Jerome noted in *Three Men in a Boat* (which, it is said, he largely completed in the town's Two Brewers Inn) is a 'bustling, lively little town' set on that part of the Thames where 'the river itself is at its best'. It is no surprise that our exploration of the town starts at the river.

It is thought that the first bridge at Marlow was built by the Knights Templar, who had a preceptory at what became Bisham Abbey. The present bridge, believed to be the third, was built in 1832 by William Tierney Clark, who also linked Buda and Pest across the Danube. From the centre of the bridge the view of the town and river is excellent. The Compleat Angler Hotel on the southern side of the bridge recalls Isaak Walton's famous book: the hotel has been popular with anglers since the 16th century.

From the town side of the bridge a lovely riverside walk heads upstream, passing Higginson Park and Court Garden House to the right. The house was built in 1760 by Dr Battie, a local physician whose specialization in mental disorders is claimed to be the origin of the word 'batty' (though others claim it derives from 'bats in the belfry'). The house and its surrounding park were presented by the town to Gen. Sir George Higginson, a Crimean War veteran and Marlow resident, to celebrate his 100th birthday. The house and park are now a leisure complex. Further down river there are fine views to Bisham Church and Bisham Abbey, the latter now the National Sports Centre.

Back at the town end of the Thames Bridge, go into the town, passing, to the right, All Saint's Church , built in 1835 on the site of a previous 11th century church. Continue along The Causeway; the elaborate memorial is to Charles Frohman, the theatrical impresario drowned when the *Lusitania* was torpedoed in May 1915. Turn left along Pound Lane, then right along Portlands Alley (almost opposite Court Garden House), following it to West Street, with its famous literary connections. Plaques at Nos 31 and 47 record the times T.S. Eliot and Thomas Love Peacock spent in Marlow, while the house beside Sir William Borlase's Grammar School was where Mary Shelley wrote *Frankenstein* while she and Percy Bysshe lived in the town before departing for Italy. Opposite the grammar school is Remnantz, an 18th century house

The Thames at Marlow

that was once part of the Royal Military College before it moved to Sandhurst. The military usage is recalled in the weather vane of the wooden clock tower/cupola of the neighbouring stables, which has a man firing a cannon.

Return along West Street to Market Place and turn right along High Street to reach the end of The Causeway. Turn left along Station Road, soon reaching Marlow Place, a superb Georgian mansion, on the left. The Old Parsonage next to the house is claimed to be Marlow's oldest building, dating, in part, from the 14th century. Turn right along St Peter's Street – the church of the name was built in 1846. Near the bottom of the street, the Two Brewers Inn lies to the left. Traditionally, the 'Swan Uppers' stop here for refreshment. Turn right along the alley opposite to return to Marlow Bridge.

To the east of Marlow the AONB includes Horton and Bloom Woods, but strangely does not include the magnificent **Burnham Beeches** which, despite the name, is a huge area of mixed wood and heath. It is the beeches which are its pride, though, the area offering superb walking among awesome specimens.

From Marlow, follow the A4155 towards Henley: Bockmer Woods to the north is a lovely stretch of beech woods. A turn left soon reaches **Medmenham** where the Abbey, founded by the Cistercians in the 13th century, was one of the centres for the Hell

Fawley Court

Fire Club after the club's founder, Sir Francis Dashwood (who we shall meet again at West Wycombe) restored it. It is now a private house.

The next turn right off the main road, at Mill End, leads to **Hambleden**, an extremely pretty village. The church has a good Norman font and some excellent Renaissance panelling, as well as a fine series of monuments, including an early 16th century brass and the tomb of Sir Cope D'Oyley in which two kneeling alabaster figures are surrounded by kneeling children. On the other side of the main road from Mill End a Romano-British villa has been excavated.

Continue along the A4155, soon reaching the entrance to **Fawley Court** on the left. The Court is named for the fallow deer which once roamed the local forest, and were probably hunted by the earliest Norman squire who built a house on the site as early as the 12th century. This house was almost destroyed during the Civil War, and the next owner commissioned Sir Christopher Wren to build another, the new one incorporating some elements of the original. It was in this new Fawley Court that William and Mary stayed on their way to their Coronation. The house was later extended but it is Wren's building, and particularly the drawing room ceiling by Grinling Gibbons, which draws the attention. The ceiling is one of Gibbons' masterpieces.

After the 1939–45 War the house was sold to the Marian Fathers, an order founded in Poland in 1673. Today, in addition to the house itself, which is magnificently furnished, there is a museum founded by one of the Fathers. This has a library of books on Polish history and a remarkable collection of 16th and 17th century Polish swords. The house is now a retreat centre, but is also open to visitors. After visiting the Court and museum, visitors may stroll through the parkland which surrounds the house – it was landscaped by Capability Brown. The park extends down to the Thames, reaching it at a point about halfway along the Henley regatta course, the 'straight mile' of Henley Reach.

From Fawley Court, continue along the A4155 to return to Henley-on-Thames.

ADDRESSES AND OPENING TIMES

STONOR PARK,
Stonor (01491 638587)

❖

OPEN: all year, Sun and Bank Holiday Mon 2–5.30pm; also
open Wed from May–Sept, same time

CHILTERN SCULPTURE TRAIL,
Cowleaze Wood, nr Watlington (01865 723 684)

❖

OPEN: all year, any reasonable time

CHILTERN VALLEY WINERY AND BREWER ,
Old Luxters, nr Fingest (01491 638330)

❖

OPEN: all year Mon–Fri 9am–6pm, Sat and Sun 10am–6pm;
closes at 5pm on all days from Oct–March

BLUE MAX MOVIE MUSEUM,
Wycombe Air Park, Clay Lane, Booker (01494 529432)

❖

OPEN: March–Nov, Wed and Sun 10am–5pm. There is often
someone at the site on other days, but ring beforehand to
check

FAWLEY COURT (Marian Fathers),
Marlow Road, Henley-on-Thames (01491 574917)

❖

OPEN: March–Oct, Wed, Thu and Sun 2–5pm; closed during
Easter and Whitsun weeks

(Opposite) The Chilterns near Chequers

The M40 motorway and the A41 linking Aylesbury to Hemel Hempstead divide the Chilterns into three segments. In this chapter we explore the central area, with tours centred on High Wycombe and Amersham.

High Wycombe

The AONB encircles High Wycombe, keeping its distance on the town's northern and south-eastern edges, but elsewhere brushing its suburbs. It is perhaps appropriate that it should touch the town, for High Wycombe's prosperity from the 17th century was based on furniture-making, particularly chairs, using wood from the Chiltern forests. Early chair-making saw independent workers operating pole lathes in huts deep in the forest, making legs and back stretchers which were sent to workshops in the town for assembly. The forest wood turners were known as bodgers, and it is ironic that the word, and the men's trade – bodging – has become a shorthand for poor workmanship as they were, in fact, highly skilled. Eventually all the work of chair making was carried out in the town factories, new designs emerging that increased the town's prosperity still further. The 'Windsor' is still Britain's most popular design of wooden dining chair, while the 'wheel back' version of the Windsor, when launched, was an instant hit, cornering three-quarters of the market. When, in 1877, Queen Victoria visited the town she was welcomed with an arch built exclusively of chairs, so proud was High Wycombe of its local industry. A photograph of that extraordinary arch, together the various designs can be seen at the town's Local History and Chair Museum. As the name implies, the museum also traces High Wycombe's origins from Roman times.

Church Square
High Wycombe

Our exploration of the town starts from the museum: cross the footbridge over the railway to the right of the entrance and turn right along Castle Street to reach All Saints', Buckinghamshire's largest church. The church was rebuilt in the 13th century and considerably

Corn Market, High Wycombe

extended – outwards and upwards – in the 15th. Inside there are several excellent memorials and a stained glass window (in the north transept) which celebrates the contribution of women to history. It is known as the Dove Window as it was presented by Dame Frances Dove, a leader of the movement to educate girls: Dame Frances was the headmistress of Wycombe Abbey girl's school and High Wycombe's first woman councillor.

Go through the churchyard to reach the Guildhall, erected in 1757 on the site of an earlier market hall. The hall was the gift to the town of William, Earl of Shelbourne, the local MP. It is surmounted by an octagonal cupola, itself topped by a wrought-iron weathervane bearing Lord Shelbourne's centaur crest. Each May beside the Guildhall, the famous 'weighing in' ceremony of the town's mayor takes place. In a ceremony dating from 1893, the outgoing mayor is weighed and the weight announced to the crowd by the town's macebearer. If the mayor's weight has gone down there is polite applause. If it has gone up there are boos and hisses as the townsfolk register their disapproval of the mayor growing fat at their expense. The new mayor is then weighed in.

Across from the Guildhall is the delightful Little Market House, built in 1761 by Robert Adam and known locally as the 'Pepper Pot'. Beyond the Guildhall is Paul's Row, the heart of the medieval town: the Tourist Information Centre lies here.

The Guildhall and Little Market House stand at the trading heart of old High Wycombe, now called Corn Market but once known as The Shambles, that being the medieval name for the place where animals were butchered and meat sold. Of the present buildings only The Antelope dates from the medieval era, being 17th century, though it now has a 19th century façade.

Bearing left from the church, Corn Market leads into High Street, which its collection of 18th and 19th century buildings. The Red Lion Hotel was the scene of Benjamin Disraeli's first political speech when in 1832 he attempted, unsuccessfully, to become the local MP. Disraeli stood under the portico topped by the Red Lion: this is not the lion which stood, dignified and aloof, above Disraeli, that having been removed to the Local History and Chair Museum for safe keeping. Close to the hotel the first Royal Military College stood before being resettled in Sandhurst.

Across the road from the Red Lion, W.H. Smith occupies a site on which Buckingham House once stood. The house, called Bob-bin Castle by the locals, was the centre of High Wycombe's lace-making industry which, in the 17th and 18th centuries, was only exceeded by chair-making in its importance to the local economy. At the end of High Street, a right turn along Queen Victoria Road leads to an open area known as The Rye where, during the Civil War, a short battle is said to have claimed the lives of over 1,000 men. A century later, in 1736, two local highwaymen were exe-cuted here on a tall gibbet, designed to improve the view for the hundreds who turned up to watch. So great was the crush that the walls surrounding the grammar school collapsed, and a good time was had by (more or less) all. In Easton Street, the continuation of High Street across the junction, there is an interesting row of almshouses, built in 1856 but in convincing mock-Tudor style.

As noted earlier, the Chilterns woodland crowds the town, and before starting the next tour it is worth exploring these fringe areas. Particularly good are Kings and Gomm's Wood to the east of the town centre. Kings in an old bodger's wood now protected not only for its trees, but for its woodland flowers – wood avens, dog violet, bird's-foot trefoil – butterflies and bird life. Gomm's Wood is now the centre of a community conservation project, with local volunteers helping to protect the flora and fauna.

Finally, before leaving High Wycombe, take the short trip north (along the A4010) to visit **Hughenden Manor**. This red brick mock Gothic house was built in the 18th century, but remodelled in 1862. It has an impressive façade, though not everyone was impressed, Pevsner calling it excruciating and aggressive. It is now most famous as the home of Benjamin Disraeli from 1847 until his death in 1881. Born in 1804 of Jewish-Italian stock, Disraeli was the local MP for almost thirty years and Prime Minister in 1868 and from 1874–80. He was made Earl of Beaconsfield in 1875. His purchase of Hughenden was assisted by friends who felt he should have a house consistent with his status. Disraeli needed the assistance as he was not a wealthy man: indeed, his roots were seemingly at odds with Toryism, yet he reconstructed the party, taking it away from Sir Robert Peel's protectionism and creating an enthusiasm for Empire. He invented 'one nation Toryism', a philosophy he outlined and expanded in three novels.

After the rigours of power Disraeli liked to return to Hughenden where he would 'saunter about the park examining the trees'. Visitors can do the same, then enjoy the garden, re-created to the original design of Disraeli's wife, Mary Anne. The house remains virtually as he left it, and includes manuscripts, letters from Queen Victoria and other personal mementoes. Disraeli was Queen Victoria's favourite Prime Minister, and she had a monument raised in the church where Disraeli and his wife are buried.

Hughenden Manor

TOUR 7: The Hell Fire Club and Chequers

This first tour of the central Chilterns covers the AONB between the M40 and the A413, visiting sites as different as the Prime Minister's country residence and the Hell Fire Club's underground meeting place.

Leave High Wycombe north-westward along the A40 towards Oxford, soon reaching **West Wycombe**, a village entirely owned by the National Trust. The estate of which the village forms part was bought by the Dashwood family in 1698, but a large part of it had been badly neglected by 1929 when it was bought and renovated by the Royal Society of Arts. The Society passed it to the National Trust in 1934 and the Trust have maintained it since that time. With its collection of houses spanning the centuries from the 16th to the 19th, West Wycombe is a showpiece English village. The Church Loft House, with its projecting first floor and curious clock, is the best of several very picturesque buildings. The village church stands on top of a hill, within the boundaries of an Iron Age hill-fort. Though medieval in origin, it was rebuilt in the late 18th century by Sir Francis Dashwood MP, one-time Chancellor of the Exchequer and founder of the Dilettanti Society, and, more famously, the Hell Fire Club. The Dilettanti Society were for those, like Sir Francis, who loved classical and Renaissance art. Quite different was the Hell Fire Club whose members are notorious for having indulged in Black Magic and alchemy, though the hard evidence for this is vague. More likely the members were fond of an uninhabited good time, their alchemy being confined to experiments on the effects of significant amounts of alcohol on the human body. The Club – the name was a later invention by outsiders, the members only referring to themselves as the Brotherhood of St Francis or Dashwood's Apostles – usually met (only twice each year, despite the stories) usually for a week or so in Medmenham Abbey between Marlow and Henley, but also in the caves Dashwood had excavated near West Wycombe. The Club's membership included Earl Sandwich, the First Sea Lord, an

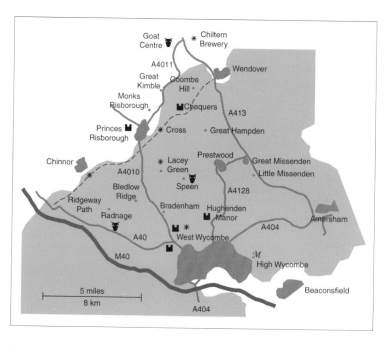

Oxford professor and the son of the Archbishop of Canterbury. At first it was a secret society – though its meetings were known to locals – but became public knowledge when John Wilkes, another MP and Club member, was imprisoned for insulting George III and leaked details in a public row with Earl Sandwich over the government policy which had provoked the insult.

On the church tower Dashwood mounted a golden ball, a copy of the one on Venice's Custom House, large enough to hold himself and a few guests. Dashwood was clearly an extrovert, with both the money and the position to indulge himself. His enthusiasm for odd places to entertain guests and Club members probably helped the stories of strange goings-on, and these were further fuelled by a heady mixture of disapproval and envy among the locals. Certainly the golden ball is curious and the church's interior – said to have been modelled on the Sun temple at Palmeyra in Syria – equally so, though there are superb carvings by Grinling Gibbons; the font, its base showing a snake catching a dove,

West Wycombe Park

sets the tone. One guest at the golden ball claimed it was the 'best Globe Tavern he had ever been in', while another claimed the guests had drunk a potent milk punch and sang songs 'unfit for the ears of the world below'. As they were above a church and the locals could doubtless hear the songs, tales of Black Magic rites were inevitable.

Beside the church is a mausoleum built of Portland Stone in 1765 by Sir Francis Dashwood for his two wives. The classical-style building, open to the sky, is modelled on Constantine's Arch in Rome. The heart of Paul Whitehead, the poet, and steward of the Hell Fire Club, is also buried here.

Dashwood remodelled **West Wycombe Park** (to the south of the village and also owned by the National Trust) in 1750, essentially rebuilding an earlier house. With its colonnaded façade in Palladian style, the house is almost as theatrical as the owner. Inside, the decorations, furnishings and artwork all date from Sir Francis' occupation. The decorations show Dashwood's love of things Italian, the ceilings being echoes of works in Renaissance *palazzos*. The park surrounding the house was landscaped by Humphrey Repton, though its naturalism is overlaid by Dashwood's classical leanings, the park being dotted with temples and sculpture.

West Wycombe Caves, close to the village, show an interesting side to Sir Francis Dashwood's character. Though willing to use his position and wealth shamelessly, he was concerned for the welfare of the villagers. When, in the late 1740s, there were a series of poor harvests, Dashwood employed the near-starving farm labourers to excavate the caves, using the chalk to create a road from West Wycombe to High Wycombe, Dashwood's road lying below the present A40. The caves, which took four years to excavate, were then used for meetings of the Hell Fire Club,

West Wycombe Park

whose members feasted in the Banqueting Hall and generally held true to the Club's motto of 'Do Whatever You Like'. As what the Club's members liked involved the company of ladies as uninhibited as themselves, the farm workers who had sweated to remove the chalk were probably as envious as they were grateful for their wages. Today the caves have tableaux depicting Dashwood and other Club members – including Paul Whitehead and John Wilkes – and visitors, the latter including Benjamin Franklin, the American diplomat/scientist.

To the south of West Wycombe there is fine walking in Hellbottom Wood, while to the north an equally fine walk through Hearnton Wood reaches **Bradenham**, another National Trust village. The manor house here was once the home of Isaac D'Israeli, father of Benjamin Disraeli. The elder Disraeli is buried in the village church, a

Dashwood's Mausoleum West Wycombe

West Wycombe Caves

neat building with a squat tower and one of the oldest Norman doorways in Buckinghamshire. The is also excellent walking in the National Trust woodland to the east of Bradenham, an area called 'Hurstly' in Benjamin Disraeli's novel *Endymion*.

Bradenham lies on the A4010 which leaves the A40 close to West Wycombe. Our route goes that way, too, but detours to the west are necessary to see the best of the woodland in this area of the Chilterns. There is no scarp-edge road between the A40 and Princes Risborough, and so the roads from Bledlow Ridge and Radnage to Chinnor must be followed to explore the area. To reach Radnage, follow the A40 towards Stokenchurch, turning right near **Horsleys Green** where Gibbons Farm is home to rare breeds of pigs, sheep and cattle. The farm dates from the early 16th century and is fascinating; there is also a picnic area. **Radnage** has a 12th century church with 13th century murals. From it an old coach road heads north-west, a road claimed to be haunted by the ghost of a highwayman.

The village of **Bledlow Ridge** is named for the chalk ridge which takes a road north-west, the name being Saxon for 'blood hill', commemorating a battle with the Danes. These north-westerly roads visit the beautiful woodland of Great Bledlow Wood. At its scarp edge is Bledlow Cross, cut into the chalk of Wain Hill. This huge cross – over 22m (75ft) across – is of unknown origin. Some say Saxon, perhaps commemorating the Bledlow Ridge battle, while others claim it is no older than 17th century. In **Chinnor**, below the cross, an old GWR branch line has been restored, and steam and diesel engines take trains from the village to the outskirts of Princes Risborough.

On the A4010, to the north of Bradenham, a right turn leads towards **Speen** where Westcroft Stables are a rest home for rescued horses and donkeys. This registered charity is open throughout the year. There is also a good pottery in the village. From Speen, follow the minor road to **Lacey Green** to view the country's oldest smock mill, built at Chesham in the mid-17th century, but moved to its current position in 1821. The mill still has its original machinery, which has been restored to working order, and is open to the public. From the windmill, regain the main road and turn right to follow it into Princes Risborough.

Princes Risborough is positioned at the head of a pass through the Chilterns, one taken by the railway and the A4010, and one that was of strategic importance from earliest times. There is local evidence of settlement from Neolithic through to Saxon times, the name Risborough first appearing in 903 when the area was still being disputed between Saxons and Danes. After the Norman Conquest the town sinks below the historical horizon – though it is known to have been the site of a Royal Stud – until the early 14th century when it was given to Edward, the Black Prince, this explaining the addition to the town's name. Tradition has it that Edward had a palace near St Mary's Church, though this may only have been a hunting lodge or a manor house beside the stud. The site of 'The Mount', as Edward's manor became known, is now occupied by the Stratton Road car park.

High Street Princes Risborough

The car park is a convenient place to start a tour of the town. On the bank opposite, which surrounds the churchyard, a plaque notes the Black Prince's connection to the town. St Mary's Church is an impressive building, dating from the 13th century, with an elegant tower and spire added in 1907 (but in Perpendicular style). Follow Church Street towards the town. To the right is the 17th century Corner Cottage, while to the left – and set back – is the Manor House. This, too, is 17th century, replacing an earlier one reputedly visited by Elizabeth I. The house was acquired and restored by the Rothschilds, and is now owned by the National Trust. The house, which has a superb Jacobean staircase, is open by prior arrangement only. Walk past the Manor House (and the church, to the left) to reach Monks Staithes, a beautiful 17th century half-timbered house which was once the vicarage. A plaque on the house notes that it was once home to Amy Johnson, the English aviator who was – among many firsts – the first woman to fly solo to Australia. Apparently she occasionally parked a plane on the grass beside the church. Amy was killed when her plane crashed into the Thames estuary, an odd coincidence being that the naval officer who dived into the river in a vain attempt to rescue her had been born in nearby Monks Risborough.

Back in Church Street, bear right, passing fine 17th/18th century houses, to reach the Market Square. The Market House was built in 1824 (though there was an earlier building) and with its arcading and bell tower is delightful. The Town Council meet on the first floor. To the left is Duke Street, worth following to see St Teresa of the Child Jesus Roman Catholic Church, its domes reminiscent of European Byzantine churches. It was built in 1937 and has wooden reliefs sculpted by Stephen Foster, who worked on Liverpool's Roman Catholic Cathedral.

Bear right into High Street and enjoy the array of fine buildings, some Georgian, others from the 19th century. At the end of the street is a memorial plaque to Lt Clyde Cosper of the USAAF who, in 1943, refused to parachute from his crippled Flying Fortress, steering it away from the town and thus saving it and the townsfolk from a dreadful impact. Bear left into Horn Lane to see the Pudding Stone, a conglomerate rock brought to the town from the Icknield Way, where it is believed to have been a waymarker. From the stone the Whiteleaf Cross, carved in the chalk of the Chilterns scarp, can be seen to the north-east.

To return to the car park, it is best to reverse the outward route, though train enthusiasts will follow Bell Street (a continuation of Horns Lane) and Station Road to reach the railway station. Apart from mainline services, the Chinnor and Princes Risborough Railway runs trains on the old branch line to Chinnor, using steam and diesel engines. Trains depart from Chinnor Station.

Leave Princes Risborough along the A4010, soon reaching side roads to **Monks Risborough** – named for its medieval ownership by Christ Church, Canterbury – on the left. The flint church here has some good early brasses, and close to it is a 16th century dovecote, square and stone-built with a pitched, tiled roof, a very elaborate building considering its usage. To the right from the A4010 there are turnings to **Whiteleaf**, a picturesque village famous for the cross carved on the chalk scarp. The age of the cross is disputed, some historians favouring a Saxon origin, others a medieval one. Above the cross is a Neolithic long barrow from which the body of a man buried, unusually, in a wooden chamber was excavated.

Our route continues along the A4010 to **Great Kimble**, where John Hampden made his stand against the Ship Money Tax in 1635. Ship Money was a medieval tax levied on coastal areas to pay for naval ships. It was discontinued, but then re-instated by Charles I, who imposed it on the whole country and in a time of peace, simply to raise revenue. Hampden is said to have ridden his

Monks Risborough

horse into the village church to voice his objections to his assembled tenants and neighbours. Charles' imposition of the tax is said by some historians to have been a major step on the path to the Civil War (*see* below).

Turn right to **Little Kimble** where the church has some excellent 14th century wall paintings. The minor road now heads for Ellesborough passing, on the right, a castle site (probably early medieval) known as Cymbeline's Castle. The tradition that this was the fortress of the 1st century AD British chieftain has been suggested as the root of the name of the Kimble villages. **Ellesborough** is a pretty village with a good church and quaint 18th century almshouses, but is more famous for the house which lies to the south. This is **Chequers**, the country residence of British Prime Ministers. In the 12th century the estate here was owned by Elias Hostiarius, the Usher of the Exchequer, and it was his title that named it (the Exchequer itself was named for a chequer-board table on which accounts were settled). There was probably a manor house in Elias' day, and certainly one in the 13th century, which Sir William Hawtrey rebuilt in the 1560s. Almost immediately it was used as a prison for Lady Mary Grey, younger sister of the ill-fated Lady Jane Grey. Mary's crime was not being Jane's sister, but marrying Thomas Keys, a porter in the Royal household. Elizabeth I was outraged, both by the pair marrying in secret and by the difference in social class between them. The queen emphasized this difference by imprisoning Keys in Fleet prison. Mary was released and re-instated at court on Keys' death.

Later the house was owned by the Russell family into which Oliver Cromwell's youngest daughter Frances married, as a result of which the house has a remarkable collection of Cromwell memorabilia. The collection is not open to the public as, hardly surprisingly, Chequers is off limits to all but official visitors. In 1917 Lord Lee of Fareham (the former Arthur Lee MP) gave the house to the nation. It is often said the gift was for the safe deliverance of the county from the perils of the 1914–18 war, though in 1917 the peril was far from over. Lee's stated reason was to allow the country's Prime Ministers to taste 'the high and pure air of the Chiltern hills and woods', the hope being that 'the more sanely they will rule'. Visitors will make their own decisions on the latter.

Though not open to the public, Chequers can be seen from public footpaths that run beside it. From Ellesborough a path runs south along the western side of the estate, linking with the Ridgeway National Trail which leads to the minor road to the east of the house; a path returns to Ellesborough from this road. There is also a good view from the summit of Coombe Hill to the east (and also on the Ridgeway). The hill can be reached by a short walk from a car park on its southern edge: turn right at Butler's Cross, then left after passing Chequers.

The memorial on **Coombe Hill** commemorates 148 Chiltern-born men who died in the Boer War. It was erected in 1904, but rebuilt in 1938 after being damaged by lightning. From the hill there is a marvellous view, not only of Chequers but also of the Vale of Aylesbury. It is often said that the hill is the highest point on the Chilterns: it is not, though it is the highest viewpoint – there is a slightly higher point buried in Wendover Woods.

Bucks Goat Centre   *The Shop, Chiltern Brewery*

Our tour continues past Chequers, but a short detour from Butler's Cross – turn left – reaches the A4010 at Terrick. Turn right here to reach the **Chilterns Brewery**, where the brewing rooms can be visited. There is also a small museum of brewing and a licensed shop selling the four beers brewed on site. Continuing along the A4010 from the roundabout at Terrick soon reaches a turn for the **Bucks Goat Centre**. Although outside the AONB, the centre, with its dozen or so breeds of goat, together with poultry, sheep, pigs, donkeys and a pets' corner, is worth visiting, especially if you have children. The centre has a farm information centre, plant nursery and offers donkey rides most weekends.

Our tour follows the minor road southwards past Coombe Hill to reach Hampden Park, the main feature of **Great Hampden**. The park was the home of John Hampden, who rode his horse to Great Kimble Church. Hampden was a cousin of Oliver Cromwell and became the local MP. He was levied twenty shillings for Ship Money and arrested and tried when he failed to pay. He lost the case, but became a national celebrity, and one known to the King, who demanded his arrest (and that of four other MPs) in 1642. This action precipitated the Civil War in which Hampden was killed fighting at Chalgrove Field, close to the Chilterns, in 1643. He was buried at the church near his house. The church has brasses to several John Hampdens as the family owned the estate for centuries, but the 'real' John's grave is unmarked; the monument to him was erected in 1743 to mark the centenary of his death. A local legend maintains that to settle a dispute on the manner of his death John Hampden was exhumed in the early 19th century. Conflicting traditions had him shot by the enemy, or killed when his own pistol exploded. The exhumation is

Wall Painting
Little Missenden Church

said to have revealed an amputated hand, suggesting the latter was correct.

Hampden House, rebuilt in the 18th century, but with earlier details, is not open to the public, but a fine walk links it, the villages of Great and Little Hampden and the Hampden Monument – which tells the story of Hampden's refusal to pay the Ship Money Tax – to east of the house. An alternative walk follows Grim's Ditch in the woodland to the west.

From Hampden, follow the minor road to **Prestwood**, a small town that was once famous for cherries, Prestwood Blacks. The town has some good old cottages and an interesting Victorian church, but as it grew up around a collection of hamlets there is no authentic old centre. Nearby **Great Missenden** is a more interesting village. Set in the Chilterns Valley and on the road from Aylesbury to London, it was a coach stop – there were once a dozen inns spread out along the High Street – and later a popular home for rich folk moving out of London. The High Street, long and gently curving, is a delight, a picturesque array of half-timbered and Georgian buildings, and one or two that are much older – the George Inn dates, in part at least, from the 15th century. Behind the inn is one of the two courthouses for the Chiltern Hundreds. The church, standing away from the village, is 14th century, but almost certainly stands on the site of a Saxon church. Inside, there is a fine Norman font and good 15th century wood carving. Below the church stands Missenden Abbey, founded for Augustinian monks in 1133. The abbey was remodelled in the 18th century, then given Gothic touches in the early 19th century. It is now an adult education centre.

Follow the A413 southwards, then take the minor road to **Little Missenden**, a pretty village with a fine church most notable for the early medieval wall paintings discovered beneath the whitewash in the 1930s. The most complete shows St Christopher carrying the Christ Child over water, but there are fragments of several others. The whole collection of paintings is the most interesting in the county.

Now follow the A413 into Amersham.

ADDRESSES AND OPENING TIMES

WYCOMBE LOCAL HISTORY AND CHAIR MUSEUM,
Priory Avenue, High Wycombe (01494 421895)

❖

OPEN: all year, Mon–Fri 10am–5pm, Sat 10am–1pm and
2–5pm

HUGHENDEN MANOR (National Trust),
High Wycombe (01494 532580)

❖

OPEN: house, March, Sat and Sun, 1–5pm, April–Oct
Wed–Sun 1–5pm (but closed Good Friday and open on Bank
Holiday Mon); garden, as house, but open 12noon–5pm;
park, all year, daily 12noon–5pm

WEST WYCOMBE PARK (National Trust),
West Wycombe (01628 488675)

❖

OPEN: house, June–Aug, Sun–Thurs 2–6pm; gardens, April
and May, Wed, Sun and Bank Holiday Mon 2–6pm,
June–Aug, Sun–Thurs 2–6pm

WEST WYCOMBE CAVES,
West Wycombe (01494 533739)

❖

OPEN: March–Oct, daily 11am–5.30pm, Nov–Feb, Sat, Sun
11am–5.30pm

GIBBONS FARM RARE BREEDS,
Bigmore Lane, Horsleys Green (01494 482385)

❖

OPEN: all year, daily 10am–6pm

THE HOME OF REST FOR HORSES,
Westcroft Stables, Slad Lane, Speen (01494 488464)
❖
OPEN: all year, daily 2–4pm

LACEY GREEN WINDMILL,
Lacey Green (01844 343560)
❖
OPEN: May–Sept, Sun and Bank Holiday Mon 2.30–5.30pm

MANOR HOUSE (National Trust),
Princes Risborough
❖
OPEN: by written arrangement with the tenant only, and then
on Wed only 2.30–4.30pm

CHINNOR AND PRINCES RISBOROUGH RAILWAY,
Chinnor Station (01844 273535,
talking timetable 01844 353535)
❖
Trains run on weekends from late March to late October;
there are normally five trains on running days

CHILTERN BREWERY,
Nash Lee Road, Terrick (01296 613647)
❖
OPEN: all year, Mon–Sat 9am–5pm

BUCKS GOAT CENTRE,
Layby Farm, Old Risborough Road,
Stoke Mandeville (01296 612400)
❖
OPEN: all year, Tues–Sun 10am–5pm
also open Bank Holiday Mon

Amersham Old Town

'A rightly pretty market town on Fryday, of one street well built with timber' said Leland, the Elizabethan traveller, after a visit to Amersham. The description is still a good one, for although there are now markets on Tuesdays and Saturdays as well as Fridays (and they are not the type of market Leland saw) and a new town has grown up to the north-east, old Amersham is still 'one street well built'.

To explore Amersham Old Town, use the Dovecote car park at the eastern end of the street. The car park lies beside the new Tesco supermarket, a stark reminder that as you head eastwards from the Old Town you leap several centuries forward in time. At the exit from the car park, bear left across London Road (as this section of the 'one street' is called) to see an old vagrancy notice (on No. 60). Old Amersham's folk clearly wanted to maintain a dignified town.

Now walk back along London Road. There are fine 17th century half-timbered houses on your left, then the Griffin Inn, a coaching inn that was old when Cromwell's soldiers took it over in 1656. Opposite the inn are the fine Memorial Gardens, opened in 1949 to commemorate the town's men who died in the 1914–18 and 1939–45 wars. From the rear of the gardens a footpath bears north-east, crossing the River Misbourne and heading uphill to the Martyrs' Memorial. Amersham was an early centre for the Reformation: as early as 1413 followers of John Wycliffe, the late 14th century Oxford lecturer, had preached barefoot in the town and been condemned to death as heretics. Despite this, Amersham remained a centre for the Lollards (as Wycliffe's followers were known) and in 1506 there was further repression; some followers were branded on the cheek with an 'L' (for Lollard) or 'H' (for Heretic), but others were burned at the stake. Legend has it that the executions took place behind the church and that for

Vagrancy Notice
Amersham Old Town

centuries nothing grew on the patch of land. The memorial remembers these religious martyrs.

On the right (as you enter) of the Memorial Gardens is the Old Malthouse, a 15th century malthouse of the monks of Missenden Abbey. On the other side of the Gardens is the town church, built in the 14th and 15th centuries, though restored in Victorian times. Inside there is some excellent 17th century stained glass and one of the finest collection of

The Church and Memorial Gardens Amersham Old Town

monuments in Buckinghamshire, most of them to members of the Drake family, lords of the manor. That of Mrs Elizabeth Drake, including a kneeling mother and six children, is the most moving; that of Thomas Tyrwhitt Drake, in which he reads, reclining in his dressing gown the most surprising. There are also a number of 15th and 16th century brasses.

Ahead now is Market Square and the Market Hall. The Hall was the gift of Sir William Drake in 1682: the arcaded ground floor was the market, the upper floor being schoolroom, courtroom and general meeting room. The Hall houses the old town water pump, dated 1782, and the old town lock-up. Continue along High Street (Amersham's street starts as London Road, becomes Broadway near the Griffin Inn and High Street after Market Square), reaching Elmodesham House on the left. This is the town's largest building, dating from the early 18th century, but

Amersham Old Town

taking its name from the Domesday name for Amersham. Almost opposite is Amersham Museum, housed in a 15th century house which retains its herb garden. The museum explores the town's history, with special exhibits on the Lollard martyrs and the 19th century cottage industries of lacemaking and straw plaiting.

Beyond the museum, to the left, are the Drake Almshouses, built in 1657 by Sir William Drake to house six poor women. Further on, to the right, are the twelve cottages of Turpin's Row, erected in 1678 and with no connection to Dick Turpin, despite a local legend linking them to the highwayman. To return to the car park, go back along High Street, turning right just beyond Elmodesham House to follow a lane (beside No. 38) to the Baptist Church, built in 1784 with a truncated roof and glazed lantern. Go past the church to reach The Platt, claimed to be Amersham's oldest street. Turn left – Chimney Cottage, to the left, is wonderfully picturesque – to reach Whielden Street.

To the right along the Street is a Friends' Meeting House built in 1685. Amersham seems to have had a history of both non-conformity and intolerance, records showing that a Quaker funeral was once broken up by a gang from the Griffin Inn who imprisoned the coffin bearers and left the coffin in the road, denying access to it for an entire day.

Turn left, soon reaching the town's Workhouse, on the right. At the road junction, turn right to return to the car park.

TOUR 8: The South-Eastern Chilterns

This short tour heads east from Amersham, taking a short circuit through the Chalfont villages to explore the south-eastern extension of the AONB.

From Amersham Old Town, drive through the new town of Amersham-on-the-Hill and take the A404 east, towards the M25. The road goes through **Little Chalfont**, a town which grew up around the railway, to reach **Chenies**, a pretty village, typically English with cottages surrounding a green, a manor house and a church. The manor house was built in the late 15th century and modified in the early 16th, and was visited by both Henry VIII and Elizabeth I. The house is furnished in Tudor style and is used to display flowers which are dried in the adjacent shop building. There are several other interesting features: the gardens include a Physic Garden, used for growing medicinal herbs, a sunken garden and areas where the flowers for the floral arrangements are grown. There is also a doll collection.

St Michael's Church, Chenies, is 15th century and houses what Pevsner considered the finest collection of monuments in an English parish church. There are brasses in the main body of the church, but the Bedford Chapel holds the real treasures. The chapel is sadly not open to the public, but can be viewed. The

Chenies Manor

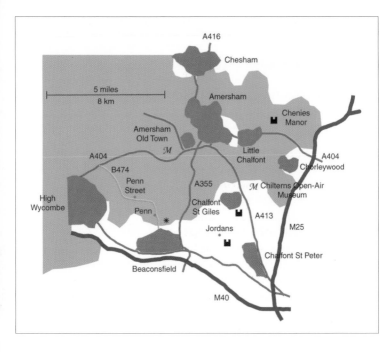

monuments are to members of the Russell family – John Russell, who died in 1555 was the first Earl of Bedford – and are masterpieces in alabaster and marble. The finest of all is that to the 5th Earl (the 1st Duke) who died in 1700.

Turn right off the A404 to **Chorleywood**. The town's name, some claim, with little justification and undoubtedly tongue very firmly in cheek, should actually be 'Charley Wood' as one or other King Charles once rested in local woods during a tiring journey. Follow a minor road south-westwards to the B4442 and turn left for Chalfont St Giles. Soon, a left turn leads to the **Chiltern Open Air Museum**. Here historic buildings from the Chilterns have been re-erected after rescue from their original sites and renovation, the buildings illustrating life in the area from the Iron Age almost to the present day. There is a regular programme of events, many aimed at children, a woodland walk, a sculpture trail, a furniture exhibition by modern craftsmen and a pets' corner. There are also a children's playground, a café and a shop. The Hawk and

Owl Trust also have an exhibition at the site, though there are no captive birds.

Return to the B4442 and turn left to reach the A413. To the right as you approach the main road is The Vache, an Elizabethan house once owned by Admiral Sir Hugh Palliser. Palliser was Captain James Cook's patron and had a Pacific Island (Ile Vache) named in his honour. To reciprocate, Palliser built an arch as a memorial to Cook. Cross the A413 to reach **Chalfont St Giles**, a lovely village lying close to the River Misbourne. The flint church is 13th century, but was remodelled in Victorian times. Inside are several good memorial brasses and some excellent 14th century murals depicting scenes from the life of the Virgin and of Christ, together with a Creation scene. The cir-

Chiltern Open Air Museum

cus owner Bertram Mills is buried in the churchyard. Close to the church is Milton's Cottage, where John Milton wrote *Paradise Lost*. In 1665, anxious to escape the plague which was sweeping London, Milton asked his friend Thomas Ellwood to find him somewhere to live. Ellwood secured this cottage, but was impris-

Milton's Cottage, Chalfont St Giles

Mayflower Barn, Jordans

oned as a Quaker before Milton moved in. On his release, Ellwood visited Milton who gave him his new work to read. It is said that Ellwood admonished Milton for paying too much attention to the loss of Paradise and ignoring its finding. Milton promptly started work on *Paradise Regained* which he completed after returning to London. The Chalfont cottage is the only house known to have inhabited by Milton and has a wealth of memorabilia of the poet and his works.

Ellwood's Quakerism is a good link with **Jordans**, which lies a short distance south of Chalfont St Giles. Old Jordans, a 17th century farmhouse, was where William Penn and other early members of the Society of Friends met. The farm is now a Quakers' hostel. William Penn, the son of Admiral Sir William Penn, was born in 1644 and imprisoned in 1668 for his writings on religion, the basis of the Society of Friends, or Quakers. Acquitted in 1670, he was granted land in North America by Charles II and founded what was to become the state of Pennsylvania and the city of Philadelphia.

Close to the farm is the Mayflower Barn, constructed in part with timbers from *Mayflower*, the ship which took the Pilgrim Fathers to North America. A short step away is the Friends' Meeting House, built in 1688, the first to be constructed after the Toleration Act allowed such buildings. In the graveyard beside it lie William Penn, his wives Gulielma and Hannah, and ten of his sixteen children, together with Isaac Pennington and Thomas Ellwood. The village of Jordans was built in 1915 by the Quakers, who hoped to establish a community in this historic and scenically beautiful spot. The attempt was not successful, but the village the Quakers founded, though enlarged, is still wonderfully picturesque and peaceful.

To the east of Jordans is **Chalfont St Peter**, which lies outside the AONB. The village was the home of the Penningtons, who were early Quakers. The tall (18m – 60ft) flint obelisk to the north of the village (near the Epilepsy Centre) is said to have been erected as a result of a chance encounter between George III and a local

Bekonscot Model Village

man. The King, having been separated from his group while hunting, is said to have asked the man where he was. The man replied that St Giles was that way, St Peter was this way, but right here was no place at all. The King therefore had the obelisk erected so that 'here' could be a proper place.

From Jordans, follow a minor road south to the A40 and turn right. Ignore the A355 heading north – this can be taken for a quick return to Amersham, passing close to **Hodgemoor Wood** (to the west of Chalfont St Giles) where tracks explore the ancient trees – but take the B474, following it through **Beaconsfield**. The town lies outside the AONB, but the older section, well separated from the new town, is worth visiting. It straddles the A40 close to where we turn off, and has some very nice Georgian buildings. Further along the B474, just beyond the railway station and off to the right, is **Bekonscot**, the world's oldest model village, built in the late 1920s/early 1930s and illustrating the rural landscape of that time, with six villages and a Gauge 1 model railway spread across a $1^1/_2$ acre site. There are picnic areas and refreshments, a children's playground and shop.

Continue along the B474, re-entering the AONB near **Penn**. The village is often associated with William Penn, the Quaker, but there is actually no link between the two, though several of Penn's grandchildren are buried in the churchyard. The church is worth visiting for a 15th century Doom, painted not on the wall but on boards, a very rare feature. French School Meadow, close to the village, recalls a school set up by Edmund Burke MP for boys orphaned by the French Revolution.

From Penn, follow minor roads north to **Penn Street** where the flag from Sir William Howe's flagship at the battle of Brest in 1794 (when the French Navy was defeated) hangs in the church. Continue northwards to the A404 and turn right along it. At the roundabout, bear left to descend Gore Hill. At the bottom, to the right, is Bury Farm, the home of Isaac and Mary Pennington. Mary's daughter, Gulielma Springett, was the first wife of William Penn. Now bear left to return to Amersham.

ADDRESSES AND OPENING TIMES

AMERSHAM MUSEUM,
49 High Street, Amersham (01494 725754/724299)
❖
OPEN: Easter–Oct, Sat, Sun and Bank Holiday Mon
2–4.30pm; also open on Wed from June–Aug, same times

CHENIES MANOR HOUSE,
Chenies (01494 762888)
❖
OPEN: April–Oct, Wed, Thurs and Bank Holidays 2–5pm

CHILTERN OPEN AIR MUSEUM,
Newland Park, Gorelands Lane,
nr Chalfont St Giles (01494 871117)
❖
OPEN: April–Oct, Tues–Fri 2–6pm, Sat, Sun and Bank
Holidays 10am–6pm (closes at 5pm in April and Oct,
10pm in June, and open daily 10am–6pm in August);
March, Sat and Sun 10am–4pm

MILTON'S COTTAGE,
Chalfont St Giles (01494 872313)
❖
OPEN: March–Oct, Wed–Sun 10am–1pm and 2–6pm; also
open on Bank Holiday Mon, same time

BEKONSCOT MODEL VILLAGE,
Warwick Road, Beaconsfield (01494 672919)
❖
OPEN: mid-Feb–Oct, daily 10am–5pm

TOUR 9: Wendover and Berkhamsted

In this short tour we continue our exploration of the central Chilterns, visiting the area between the A413 and the A41.

Leave Amersham Old Town westwards, joining the A413 and heading north to Great Missenden. Turn right along the B485, then left to reach South Heath – reputedly haunted by a ghostly coach and four. Continue along the minor road through Ballinger Common, where productive cherry orchards once grew, to reach **The Lee**, once the home of Sir Arthur Liberty, founder of the famous store. In the 1920s the family bought the Victorian warship *Admiral Lord Howe*, using its timbers to create the famous façade of the Liberty shop on London's Regent Street. The two-ton figurehead from the ship (of Lord Howe himself) was erected at the entrance to the family home, and there it still stands, surely the strangest landmark in the entire Chilterns.

Follow the minor road through Lee Gate and Kingsash, descending to join the A413. Turn right into **Wendover**. Though the name is probably Celtic, deriving from the fast running streams – the white water – that sprang from the base of the scarp slope, and though the gap in the Chilterns is an obvious place for a settlement, little is known of the town's history before the Norman Conquest. King John granted a market and Edward I recognized the town's importance by granting it a Member of Parliament. Centuries later John Hampden, whose protest against the Ship Money Tax sparked the Civil War (*see* Tour 7), was the town's MP. Another famous Wendover MP was Edmund Burke, the famous political emancipator. When he was elected in

*Earl Howe Figurehead
The Lee*

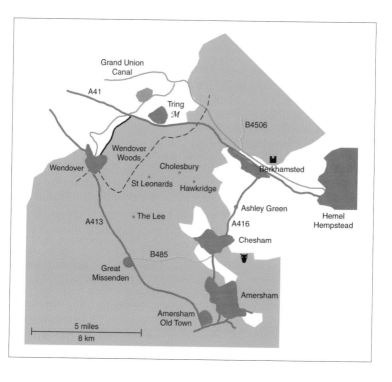

1765 he celebrated his victory in style, writing to a friend 'Yesterday I was elected for Wendover, got very drunk, and this day have an heavy cold'. Burke's method of celebrations may be seen as fairly conventional, but his description of a hangover is very unconventional and set a trend which continues to this day.

The Ridgeway National Trail enters Wendover by crossing the railway line close to the station and following Pound Street towards the town. To explore this elegant, gracious town we shall follow the Trail. To the left in Pound Street as you walk away from the railway is the Shoulder of Mutton. An inn has stood here since the early 17th century: it became the Railway Hotel to celebrate the coming of steam in 1892, but has reverted to its older name. To the right are some fine 17th century cottages.

At the cross-roads, go ahead into High Street. Soon, to the right, is Bosworth House, built in the 16th century and still possessing

Cold Harbour Cottages, Wendover

its Tudor chimneys. Beyond, to the left and right, there are fine 16th and 17th centuries houses. Of these, the most interesting is the Red Lion Hotel built in about 1620. Oliver Cromwell spent a night here in 1642 and Robert Louis Stevenson did the same in 1875. Stevenson's stay inspired him to write *An Autumn Effect*.

At the bottom of the High Street, the National Trail turns right along the shady Heron Path. That is our route too, but first we shall take a short detour. Ahead is the Clock Tower, built in 1842 as a Market Hall. The tower and spire were added in 1870 and the building then acted as the village lock-up and, later, the fire station. It now houses the Tourist Information Office. Inside, look for the grooves cut low down in the walls to allow room for the hubs of the horse-drawn fire engine. Around the corner from the Clock Tower, the Old Corner House, on the left, was once a coaching inn. The House stands at the start of Aylesbury Road, a worthwhile extension of the walk (*see* below). To the right is Tring Road which most definitely should be visited. To the right just after crossing the stream is the Old Mill, where, in the 17th century, an over-shot waterwheel ground flour. Further on, also to the right,

Bank Farm dates, in part, from the 15th century and is the town's oldest secular building. Beyond, to the left, are Cold Harbour Cottages, a beautiful and picturesque row of black and white thatched cottages reputedly given to the Boleyn family by Henry VIII as part of a royal dowry for Anne Boleyn.

Now return to Heron Path and follow it (and the National Trail) past Bucksbridge House, to the left, to reach St Mary's Church, a sturdy 14th century building. Inside there is brass monument to William Bradschawe, who died in 1537, and his wife which includes figures not only of the pair, but also of their nine children, together with the names of their twenty-three grandchildren. Now reverse the last few metres of the walk, bearing left at the fork and crossing a track to reach the cricket field. Bear left to reach South Street just beyond the pond and turn right to return to the cross-roads reached earlier.

The extension of the Wendover Walk will be of particular interest to canal lovers. From the Clock Tower, follow Aylesbury Road to reach Wharf Road, on the right. Just beyond here, to the left, is what is claimed to be the largest surviving windmill in England, built around 1800, but losing its sails in 1904. The mill is 23m (76ft) high. Follow Wharf Road to reach the Wendover Arm of the Grand Union Canal. The canal was opened in 1797, dug primarily to provide water to the Aylesbury Arm of the Grand Union, but also to assist local traders. In 1799 John Wescar, a local farmer, became the first to use a canal to carry cattle. Despite this early success, the Wendover Canal was dogged by leakage problems which meant that far from supplying the Grand Union with

Aylesbury Road
Wendover

Grand Union Canal Wendover

water it was actually draining it. For over a hundred years attempts were made to stop the leaks, draining and resealing the canal, but in 1904 the struggle was lost and the canal abandoned. Then, in 1994, Buckinghamshire County Council opened the canal towpath to walkers who can follow its 11km (6³/₄miles) to the Grand Union.

Wendover is also a good centre for woodland walking. The Ridgeway National Trail can be followed southwards from Pound Street, crossing Bacombe Hill through ash and hazel stands to reach Coombe Hill. There are also several car parks in Wendover Woods to the east of the town. The Woods, owned by the Forestry Commission, are a mix of deciduous and conifer, and are home to the *glis glis*, the edible dormouse (which is found only in a few local sites) and the firecrest, a rare (and elusive and small) bird. The Commission has a number of car parks in the wood from which waymarked trails lead out. The car parks lie close to the road followed by our tour.

To continue the tour, leave Wendover along the A4011, heading north-east to reach a minor road, on the right, for Buckland Common and Cholesbury. Before turning here, a detour is worthwhile, following the main road to **Tring**, a pleasant town where the Walter Rothschild Zoological Museum has four thousand specimens from fleas to large mammals, a remarkable collection. Tring Park, to the south of the town, lies within the AONB. The 300-acre park surrounds the Rothschild Mansion, designed by Sir Christopher Wren. It was here, in 1902, that Walter Rothschild first introduced the edible dormouse.

Turn right off the A4011. Soon a road on the right leads to the Forestry Commission car parks in Wendover Woods, though a car park for the north-eastern section of the woods is further along on the left. The first village beyond the woods is **St Leonards**, where the pretty little church has two strange monuments. That to General Cornelius Wood has a cherub sitting on a cannonball, an odd juxtaposition, while that to Seth Wood and his wife includes their sad daughters.

Continue through Buckland Common to **Cholesbury**, a village set at the edge of a large Iron Age hill-fort. Part of the village, including St Lawrence's Church, lies within the fort. Just beyond the village is an old windmill, now a private house. Several minor roads lead to Chesham from Cholesbury, each passing through fine country, but the best follows a Chiltern ridge to **Hawridge** where St Mary's Church is flint and brick with a wooden bell-tower. Hawridge Court stands within another ancient earthwork, perhaps a precursor of the much large Cholesbury Camp.

The minor road now runs just below the ridge top before swinging into Chesham Vale: continue into **Chesham**. The town lies outside the AONB, which approaches (seemingly cautiously) on the northern and south-eastern edges. The site, neatly set in the valley of the River Chess, has a long history, extending back to pre-Roman times, though the town enters recorded history only in 970 when it is mentioned in the will of Lady Elgiva, the Saxon King Edwy's divorced wife. Elgiva is now the name of the town's theatre, a small but progressive place. The best part of the town is the old heart, close to St Mary's Church. The church is medieval but Victorian-restored. Inside

Wendover Woods

there is a medieval mural of St Christopher wading through water and a touching monument to Nicholas Skottowe. The churchyard has a mausoleum to the Lowndes family: William Lowndes, Secretary to the Treasury in the early 18th century, was responsible for The Bury, the fine house to the south-west of the church, at the bottom of Church Street. To the north of the church is Lowndes Park. It was here that the windmill which now stands at Lacey Green was first built in 1650.

From Chesham it is a short journey south to Amersham, or the A416 can be followed north towards Berkhamsted. A worthwhile detour follows the B4505 towards Hemel Hempstead, then turns off, as signed, to reach **Allsorts Farm**, a pick-your-own soft fruit farm which also has a collection of rare poultry breeds (chickens, ducks and pheasants) and a pets' corner with piglets, lambs, goats and llamas.

From the farm, return to the B4505 and follow the minor road north to **Ashley Green**, a pretty village unfortunately cut in two by the main road. Turn right to reach Berkhamsted.

ADDRESSES AND OPENING TIMES

WALTER ROTHSCHILD ZOOLOGICAL MUSEUM,
Akeman Street, Tring (01442 824181)
❖
OPEN: all year, Mon–Sat 10am–5pm, Sun 2–5pm

ALLSORTS FARM,
Botley Road, nr Chesham (01494 773947/778700)
❖
OPEN: May–Oct, daily except Mon 10am–5.30pm

(Opposite) High Street, Berkhamsted

THE
NORTHERN
CHILTERNS

Finally we reach the northernmost section of the AONB, the upland between the Grand Union Canal and the conurbation of Dunstable and Luton. It is here, many would argue, that the Chilterns are at their finest: in the beautiful woodland of the National Trust's Ashridge holdings and on Ivinghoe Beacon, where the Ridgeway National Trail ends. Our exploration of the area starts from Berkhamsted.

Berkhamsted

The strategic importance of the pass through the Chilterns which the Berkhamsted site guards was recognized very early: the Romans built a road through the pass and the Saxons had a settlement here. At the time of the Conquest, Berkhamsted was so important that it was here that William came to accept the Saxon surrender before moving on to London to be crowned. William gave the town to his half-brother Robert de Mortain, confirming its importance. Robert built a motte and bailey castle at the town: the castle was later expanded into one of the most unusual and formidable defensive sites in England. Henry I held a court at the castle in 1123, and for ten years from 1155 Thomas à Becket occu-

Berkhamsted Castle

pied it as Henry II's Chancellor. Later, the French king was imprisoned at the castle after his capture at Poitiers, the Black Prince honeymooned there with his bride Joan, the Fair Maid of Kent, and Geoffrey Chaucer became the castle's Clerk of Works.

With such a central role in English history, it is no surprise that Berkhamsted is worth a visit, or that the castle is a worthwhile starting point. The earliest castle had a wooden keep; this was soon replaced with stone, and a huge curtain wall, 2m (7ft) thick, was added, creating an inner bailey at the foot of the mound. There was a moat outside this wall, then another defensive wall, in part stone, in part an earth embankment outside of which there was a second moat – Berkhamsted is unique in having two moats. The modern entrance to the site is along a causeway constructed where the original bridged and drawbridged entranceway would have been. In the mid-15th century the castle fell into disrepair, and it was subsequently used as a convenient quarry by the locals. Today, only sections of the curtain wall and the ruins of the original motte and stone keep remain. When first thrown up, the motte would have been almost 20m (60ft) high.

Leave the castle and turn right, then left through the tunnel beneath the railway. Bear right along Lower Kings Road, soon crossing the Grand Union Canal, built in the last decade of the 18th century as part of the great waterway linking London to Birmingham. Continue to the T-junction with High Street. To the right along High Street, on the left, just beyond Cowper Road, are the Sayers Almshouses, built in the late 17th century for six poor widows by John Sayer, one-time head cook to Charles II.

Turn left along the High Street, which follows the course of the old Roman road. To the right, the library in Kings Road houses the town's Tourist Information Office. To the left is the imposing Town Hall, built in Victorian Gothic style in 1860. Further on, to the right, are the Kings Arms and the Swan Inn, two old coaching inns. The Swan, dating from the 17th century, is a century older than its near neighbour. Also on the right, just beyond Chesham Road, is Dean Incent's House, a magnificent 16th century half-timbered house with an overhanging top storey. The house is

Grand Union Canal, Berkhamsted

named for John Incent, Dean of St Paul's, who founded Berkhamsted Grammar School. John's father, Robert Incent, owned the house when he was secretary to Cicely, Duchess of York, the last royal resident of the castle.

Opposite Dean Incent's House are the town's Elizabethan Court House and St Peter's church, an elegant early 13th century building. Inside there are some fine memorial brasses. Turn next left along Castle Street and walk past Chapel Street, to the right, to reach Berkhamsted School, founded by John Incent in 1544. The father of Graham Greene, the best British novelist never to win the Nobel Prize, was headmaster in the 1920s. Castle Street leads to Station Road: turn left to return to the castle.

TOUR 10: The Northern Chilterns

This final tour of the Chilterns explores that section of the AONB which lies north of the Grand Union Canal.

From Berkhamsted head north-westwards along the High Street, then turn right along the B4506 towards Dunstable. Soon this road passes through the woodland of Northchurch Common, the first of the National Trust's parcels of land in this beautiful part of the Chilterns. From the common north to Ivinghoe Beacon, and from Aldbury almost to the eastern edge of the AONB, this section of the Chilterns forms the **Ashridge Estate**, now almost entirely owned by the National Trust, an area of 15sq km (6sq miles) of commons and woodland.

In the late 13th century Edmund, the son of Richard, Earl of Cornwall, acquired two phials of Holy Blood. Richard, returning to England from a Crusade in 1242, had feared for his life when his ship was caught in a storm off the Scilly Isles, and promised to build and endow a monastery if he was spared. He was, and built his monastery at Hailes in Gloucestershire. Later, it is believed, Edmund visited the German court and was given drops of Holy Blood that had been presented to Charlemagne centuries earlier. Whatever their provenance, Edmund gave one phial to Hailes, and to house the second built a monastery here on his

Bridgewater Monument

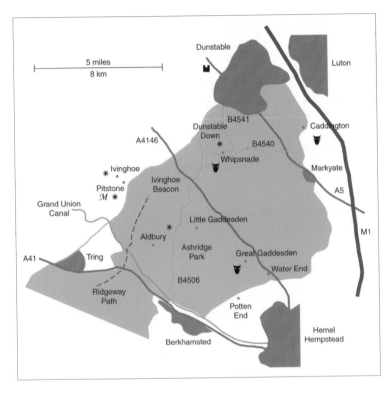

Ashridge estate. Unusually, the monastery was for monks of the Augustinian Bon Hommes, a French order. Aided by the Holy Blood, which brought many pilgrims, the monastery became rich. The Black Prince reputedly presented it with a table inlaid with gold, silver, rubies, emeralds, sapphires and pearls. But at the Dissolution all the treasures were confiscated, the Holy Blood was exposed as a fake and the monastery was given to Princess Elizabeth, the daughter of Henry VIII and Anne Boleyn – the future Elizabeth I. On the Queen's death, the monastery passed to Sir Thomas Egerton, whose descendants became the Dukes of Bridgewater, one of whom had the monastery demolished and a new house built using John Wyatt as architect. Pevsner calls

Wyatt's house 'spectacular', though others have been less kind, referring to it as a wedding cake.

The estate was eventually sold to settle death duties, most of the land becoming National Trust property and the house becoming a management college. The Trust has a Visitor Centre close to the **Bridgewater Monument** – turn left from the B4506, north of the turn to Aldbury. The Centre has information on walks in the woods and on its spectacular wildlife, which includes fallow and muntjac deer, and the rare lesser-spotted woodpecker. The monument, a granite column, was erected in 1832 to commemorate the 3rd Duke of Bridgewater who, in 1761, built one of England's first canals to carry coal from his Lancashire mines to Manchester. The canal was a huge commercial success and heralded England's canal age. The Duke is rightly seen as the 'Father of the Canal Age' but was thoroughly disliked by the locals, who claimed he was 'a wicked old bugger'. He apparently delighted in destroying flowers, had no time for the scenic delights of Ashridge – it was largely his neglect that necessitated the demolition of the old monastery buildings – preferring the industrial townscape of his northern estates, and was a passionate misogynist (perhaps as a result of being jilted by a fiancée). It is ironic that his one undoubted achievement is commemorated in the estate he found so unpleasant.

The National Trust Visitor Centre is a detour from our route, which turns left off the B4506 to reach **Aldbury**, a picturesque village – one of the prettiest in Hertfordshire – with a pond and the old stocks. Beside the pond is the Old Manor House, a marvellous 18th century timbered building. The church is early 14th century and has a lovely, slender tower. Inside there is a fine tomb to Sir Robert Whittingham, who died in 1471, and his wife, the pair lying in effigy on a tomb chest. There are also some good brasses. Elsewhere in the village, be sure to see the 18th century almshouses in Stocks Road.

From Aldbury follow the minor road northwards, passing close to the Bridgewater Monument, to the right, and Stocks, a large house to the left. This was once the home of Mrs Humphrey Ward,

Aldbury

the Victorian novelist, whose nephews Julian and Aldous Huxley were frequent visitors. We now cross from Hertfordshire into Buckinghamshire: continue along the road to reach a car park, to the left, near the high point. The Ridgeway National Trail crosses the road here and can be followed south-westwards for about 1km ($^2/_3$ mile) to reach Pitstone Hill, an excellent section of open downland – though the view north is marred by the cement works – where Neolithic flint mines have been uncovered.

Now continue along the minor road to reach the B488. A left turn here soon followed by a right turn leads to **Pitstone**, where the church houses the oldest brass in Buckinghamshire, an early 14th century memorial to a lady. The brass is just 30cm (12in) long. Follow the minor road to reach Pitstone Green Farm, on the right. Here, the farm museum has a remarkable collection of rural and domestic items from the old way of life. There are also occasional craft fairs with Morris dancers and tractor rides.

Turn right at the roundabout to reach **Ivinghoe**, an attractive village whose name was reputedly the inspiration for the name of Sir Walter Scott's *Ivanhoe*. The village is memorable for its church, a big 13th century building with a crossing tower. Inside there is a fine Jacobean pulpit and some good brasses, while in the churchyard, look for the fire hook, used to pull burning thatch off cottages in medieval times in order to stop the spread of the blaze. To the north of the church at Ford End – along the B488 towards Leighton Buzzard and on the left –is a restored water mill. Built in 1798, but almost certainly a mill site for many years before, the mill was restored in 1963 and is still occasionally used for milling.

A mill using a different power source lies to the south of the village. The Pitstone windmill is claimed to be Britain's oldest surviving post mill, some of its timbers being dated to 1627. (However, some are also inscribed 1749, leading experts to wonder if the latter is the real construction date, using timbers from an earlier mill.) Post mills were mounted on a control post, the miller using the tail pole and wheel to face the sails into the wind. Unfortunately, in 1902 a freak storm hit the mill from behind: the sails turned the wrong way and the mill gearing was destroyed. In 1937 the National Trust acquired the mill and it has been carefully restored.

From Ivinghoe, take the B489 towards Dunstable, then turn right to reach a car park for **Ivinghoe Beacon**, famous as the end (or start) of the Ridgway National Trail and for its spectacular views, the panorama including the Chilterns, Dunstable Downs and Bedfordshire plain. It is a short (about $1^{1}/_{2}$ km – 1 mile) uphill walk from the car park, but well worth the effort. From the Beacon car park, continue along the minor road to reach the B4506 at Ringshall. The Ashridge Estate Visitor Centre can be reached by turning right here. From Ringshall, a short detour leads to **Little Gaddesden** where the church houses the rich tombs of many of the Egerton family (the Dukes of Bridgewater). One is to Francis Henry Egerton, the 8th Earl of Bridgewater, who is said to have dressed his numerous cats and dogs in fashionable clothes and had them eat at his table like proper guests.

At the entrance to the Ashridge

Pitstone Green Windmill

Looking north-west from Ivinghoe Beacon

Estate is the timber-framed house of John of Gaddesden, a noted healer, who is believed to have been Chaucer's inspiration for the Doctor of Physick in *Canterbury Tales*. Chaucer would also have been delighted with Rosina Massey, a local witch, who reputedly not only flew on a broomstick in conventional witch fashion, but sent a three-legged stool on errands.

Our tour continues by following the B4506 northwards. Cross the A4146 and them turn left along the B4540 to reach **Whip-snade**. The Wild Animal Park, run by the London Zoological Society, is now much more than a conventional zoo. The collection of animals, which has recently been extended with lemurs, hippopotamus and Nepalese rhinoceros, is one of the finest in Britain, and the new theories on the conservation and showing of animals mean that they are housed and displayed in more sympathetic ways. The site is vast – over 600 acres – a narrow gauge railway helping visitors to see elephants and other large herd animals in more natural settings than were once the norm. The site includes an adventure playground for children and excellent refreshment centres.

Close to the Animal Park is the village of Whipsnade, which has a church with a 16th century brick tower. Nearby is the National Trust's Tree Cathedral, numerous species of trees planted in the shape of Liverpool Cathedral, the nave and transepts being grassed avenues. The trees were planted in the 1930s by Edmund Blyth as a memorial to three friends killed in the 1914–18 War. Services are held here occasionally in the summer.

From Whipsnade village, continue along the B4540, then turn left along the B4541 to reach a car park and Visitor Centre on the left, from where the **Dunstable Downs** can be explored. The Downs are a last section of chalk downland and offer excellent walking and views. At the southern end of the Downs are a group of Bronze Age round barrows called the Five Knolls. Excavations here also unearthed Saxon skeletons with their hands tied behind their backs, lending credence to an ancient legend that a gallows stood on the spot.

Dunstable, a modern town, but with a fascinating old centre, lies below the Downs. A tour of the old town is a must for anyone with an interest in Tudor England, and the tour should definitely start at the Priory Church of St Peter. Dunstable Priory was founded in 1131 by Henry I for Augustinian monks, and it was here in 1533 that Thomas Cranmer, Archbishop of Canterbury, held his tribunal into the legality of Henry VIII's marriage to Catherine of Aragon. Catherine refused to acknowledge the tribunal and would not come to Dunstable: she was therefore not present on 23 May when Cranmer announced (in the Lady Chapel, later demolished) the annulment of the royal marriage and

The Tree Cathedral Whipsnade

Wild Animal Park, Whipsnade

the legitimacy of Henry's marriage to Anne Boleyn, which had already taken place, secretly, the previous January. Henry had brought Anne Boleyn to the town in 1532 – he also later brought Catherine Howard and Catherine Parr on honeymoon – but his enthusiasm for the town and the priory did not save it at the Dissolution. The church was saved, originally with the intention of its becoming a cathedral. It is a glorious building with a collection of fine monuments and good stained glass.

From the church, go through the ruined priory gatehouse and across Priory Meadow to reach High Street South beside Priory House (to the right), the 13th century priory guesthouse. Turn left, soon passing the Saracen's Head, a 16th century building that is the town's oldest coaching inn. Go past Wood Street, to the left, to reach the Cart Almshouses, built in 1743 by Mrs Jane Cart. Mrs Cart was the daughter of Thomas Chew, who built the house next door, in 1715, as a school for forty boys.

Now return along the High Street, soon crossing to bear left along Ashton Square. Beyond the crossroads, Middle Row lies to the right. These old buildings stand on the site of Dunstable's medieval market. The original market stalls were replaced by permanent buildings in the 16th century. Continue to a T-junction with West Street: to the left here a plaque marks the site of the town's stocks and whipping post. Turn right, then first left along High Street North. To the left after a short distance is a restored archway which is believed to have lead to the White Horse Inn. On a visit to Dunstable in August 1537, Henry VIII rode past the Priory and stayed at this inn. The distraught Prior, fearing it meant the end for the Priory, asked Thomas Cranmer to persuade the King to stay at the Priory's guesthouse, as he had before. But to no avail.

Further on, also on the left, is the Eleanor's Cross shopping precinct, named for a cross placed at a resting point on the journey of Queen Eleanor's coffin from Lincoln to London in 1290. Almost opposite is the Old Sugar Loaf, another coaching inn, this one dating from 1717. Now return along the High Street, turning left along Church Street to regain the Priory Church.

From Dunstable, head south-eastwards along the A4, the Roman Watling Street, soon turning left along a minor road to **Caddington**, a large village on top of Blows Down. The church here has Anglo-Saxon and early Norman details. Continue south-eastwards, soon reaching the **Woodside Wild Fowl Park** near Slip End. This is one of Britain's largest poultry centres with over ninety breeds, together with many breeds of duck, geese, pheasants and swans. There are also owls and other birds of prey. The site has a farm shop and a cafe.

Now go along the B4540 to **Markyate**, once an important stop on the coaching route to London that followed the line of Watling Street. A Benedictine nunnery known as Markyate Cell was set up

Chew House, Dunstable

in the town, but after the Dissolution it became a manor house. When the coaching trade was at its height the last of the Ferrers family, lords of the manor, married a young woman called Katherine. Legend has it that Katherine was bored by her marriage to an older man, and to liven it up took to dressing as a man and robbing the local coaches. Often, it is said, her servants would find her horse in the stable covered with a lather, implying midnight rides, though her secret was never discovered (or, perhaps, revealed). Eventually one passenger she attempted to rob fired at his attacker. Katherine Ferrers managed to ride back to Markyate Cell, but collapsed at the door of her bedroom and died soon after. The 1950s film *The Wicked Lady*, starring James Mason and Margaret Lockwood, was based on Katherine Ferrers' story. Her ghost, astride a ghostly black horse, is said to haunt this section of the A5.

From Markyate, follow minor roads south-westward through the extremity of the AONB to reach the A4148 and **Water End**, a picturesque hamlet beside the River Gades. To the north of the hamlet are Gaddesden Place, built by James Wyatt for Thomas Halsey in 1773, and the Golden Parsonage, a manor house since Tudor times at least, though the present house dates from 1705. It, too, belonged to the Halsey family whose monuments can be seen in the church at **Great Gaddesden**. The church is interesting for having been built, in part, with bricks from a Roman villa. Inside there are several good brasses and monuments. To the south-west of the village, off the road to Nettleden, **Longford Children's Farm** has a pets' corner with horses, donkeys, pigs, sheep, goats, rabbits, guinea pigs and poultry. There is a farm shop and café.

From Great Gaddesden follow the road to Nettleden and Frithsden, villages that were once famous for their black cherry orchards, then head for Berkhamsted. One last detour bears left at a road junction to reach **Potten End**, another very picturesque village, just a short distance from Hemel Hempstead. Back at the road junction, continue southwards, crossing Grim's Ditch, which is very pronounced here, then passing through a final section of Chiltern woodland before reaching Berkhamsted.

ADDRESSES AND OPENING TIMES

BERKHAMSTED CASTLE (English Heritage)
(01442 871737 [keyholder])
❖
OPEN: all year, daily 10am–4pm

ASHRIDGE ESTATE (National Trust)
(01442 842062)
❖
OPEN: estate, all year, any reasonable time;
Bridgewater Monument, visitor centre and shop,
Easter–Oct, Mon–Thur and Good Friday 2–5pm,
Sat, Sun and Bank Holiday Mon 2–5.30pm

PITSTONE GREEN FARM,
Vicarage Road, Pitstone (01296 661997)
❖
OPEN: Bank Holiday Mon 2–5pm; craft fairs, June–Sept, 2nd
Sunday of Month 11am–5pm

FORD END WATERMILL,
Station Road, Ivinghoe (01582 600391)
❖
OPEN: May–Sept, Sun and Bank Holiday Mon 2.30–5.30pm
(milling only on certain Sundays – ring for details)

PITSTONE WINDMILL (National Trust),
Ivinghoe (01582 872303)
❖
OPEN: June–Aug, Sun and May Bank Holiday Mon
2.30–6pm

WHIPSNADE WILD ANIMAL PARK,
Whipsnade, nr Dunstable (0990 200123)
❖
OPEN: Feb–Easter and Oct, daily 10am–dusk;
Easter–September, Mon–Sat 10am–6pm, Sun and Bank
Holidays 10am–7pm

WHIPSNADE TREE CATHEDRAL (National Trust),
Whipsnade, nr Dunstable
(01494 528051 [NT Regional Office, for information])
❖
OPEN: any reasonable time

VISITOR CENTRE,
Dunstable Downs (01582 608489)
❖
OPEN: April–Sept, Tues–Sat 1–4.40pm,
Sun and Bank Holidays 12noon–6pm;
Oct–March, Sat, Sun and Bank Holidays 12noon–4pm

WOODSIDE WILD FOWL PARK,
Mancroft Road, Ship End (01582 841044)
❖
OPEN: all year, Mon–Sat 8am–5.30pm;
closed Christmas Day, Boxing Day and New Year's Day

LONGFORD CHILDREN'S FARM,
St Margarets, Great Gaddesden (01442 843471)
❖
OPEN: all year, daily 9am–5pm

FACTFILE

Tourist Offices

The Berkshire Downs and Chilterns lie within the southern area of the English Tourist Board, with a head office at:

Southern Tourist Board, 40 Chamberlayne Road,
Eastleigh SO50 5JH (01703 620006)

The Marlborough Downs (and the whole of Wiltshire) lie within the borders of the West Country Tourist Board, with a head office at:

West Country Tourist Board, 60 St David's Hill,
Exeter EX4 4SY (01392 425426)

Other offices are listed below; these offices are open all year:

Berkhamsted
Town Library, Kings Road, Berkhamsted HP4 3BD (01442 877638)

Devizes
39 St John's Street, Devizes SN10 1BL (01380 729408)

Didcot
The Car Park, Station Road, Didcot OX11 7AU (01235 813243)

Dunstable
The Library, Vernon Place, Dunstable LU5 4HA (01582 471012)

Henley-on-Thames
Town Hall, Market Place, Henley-on-Thames RG9 2AQ
(01491 578034)

High Wycombe
Paul's Row, High Wycombe HP11 2HQ (01494 421892)

Marlborough
George Lane Car Park, Marlborough SN8 1EE (01672 513989)

Marlow
31 High Street, Marlow SL7 1AU (01628 483597)

Newbury
The Wharf, Newbury RG14 5AS (01635 678962)

Reading
Town Hall, Blagrave Street, Reading RG1 1QH (0118 956 6226)

Wallingford
Town Hall, Market Place, Wallingford OX10 0EG (01491 826972)

Wendover
The Clock Tower, High Street, Wendover HP22 6DU (01296 696759)

Town Data

Amersham: the Old Town lies to the south-west of Amersham on the Hill and close to main roads to Aylesbury, High Wycombe and Berkhamsted. The M25 motorway (Junction 18) lies to the east. There is a train station at the western end of Amersham on the Hill. There is no bus station, but buses link with High Wycombe and Berkhamsted. There is a convenient car park at the eastern end of the Old Town's High Street.

Berkhamsted: the town lies on the A41 linking Aylesbury and Hemel Hempstead. Junctions 7 and 8 of the M1, near Hemel Hempstead, are just a few miles to the east. The train station lies close to the castle. There is no bus station, but buses between Aylesbury and Hemel Hempstead stop in the town. There is a convenient car park off Lower Kings Road, the road to the station and castle from the High Street.

Dunstable: the town lies close to the M1 motorway (Junction 11). There is no train station, but trains do stop at nearby Luton (a short distance to the east). There is no bus station in the town, but there are regular buses to Luton and Milton Keynes. There is a convenient car park in Vernon Place, close to the library/Tourist Information Office.

Henley-on-Thames: the town lies on main roads linking Reading (and the M4) with High Wycombe (and the M40), and close to Maidenhead (and the A423[M] 'extension' of the M4). There is a branch line linking the town to the main line train station at Twyford. There is no bus station, but buses do run to Reading, High Wycombe and Maidenhead.

FACTFILE

High Wycombe: the town is served by Junction 4 of the M40 motorway. The train station lies to the north-east of the town centre, while the bus station is near the Octagon Centre, close to the town centre. There is also convenient car parking at the Octagon Centre.

Oxford: the city lies close to the M40 motorway (which passes to the east – Junctions 7 and 8) and also has a dual carriageway link (the A34) southwards to the M4 (Junction 13). There is a bus station at Gloucester Green, near the main Tourist Information Office. The train station lies to the west of the city centre, on the A420 to Swindon. Parking close to the centre of the city is reasonable, with a multi-storey car park close to the Westgate Shopping Centre. There are also Park and Ride car parks on the four sides of the city.

Marlborough: the M4 motorway passes to the north of the town, the A345 linking Junction 15 to the town. There are no train or bus stations in the town, but buses link Marlborough with Swindon and Great Bedwyn, each of which is on a main train line. There is also a bus station in Swindon. Car parking is available in the High Street and close to the Tourist Information Centre, which lies to the south of the High Street.

Marlow: the town lies close to the A423(M) 'extension' of the M4 motorway, which terminates near Maidenhead, a short distance to the south, and also to the M40 which runs to the north (Junction 4). There is a branch line link to Maidenhead and main line train services. The station lies to the east of the town centre. There is no bus station, but there are regular services to High Wycombe and Maidenhead.

Newbury: the M4 motorway lies to the north of the town, the A34 dual carriageway linking Junction 13 with Newbury. The bus and train stations are close together, situated to the south of the town centre. There is a convenient car park beside the Tourist Information Centre/Town Museum.

Princes Risborough: the town lies where the A4129 road from Thame joins the A4010 (Aylesbury–High Wycombe) road. There is a train station to the south-west of the town centre and another at nearby Monks Risborough. There is no bus station, but the town lies on the route of the regular Aylesbury–High Wycombe service.

Reading: the town lies close to the M4 motorway (Junction 12 serves the western town, Junction 11 the centre and Junction 10 – the A329(M) 'extension' – the east). There are bus and train stations a short distance to the north of the Tourist Information Office and town centre. There is a convenient car park close to the train station.

Wallingford: the town lies close to main roads linking Oxford and Didcot with Reading and Henley-on-Thames. There is no train or bus station, but buses do run to the train station at Didcot, and to Oxford. There is a convenient car park near the castle ruins.

Wendover: the town is bypassed by the A413 linking Aylesbury with Amersham. There is a train station to the west of the High Street. There is no bus station, but buses connect with Aylesbury. There is car parking in the High Street.

For the sites given below 'specified times' means that the site is open only at specific times of the day or of the year. These are as indicated at the end of each chapter. 'Any time' means that access is unrestricted.

Antiques

There are a number of antique dealers in the area covered by the book, mostly concentrated in the larger towns of the Chilterns, particularly at Wallingford. There are also dealers in the towns surrounding the Downs, particularly Hungerford. There are also dealers in Oxford.

The Thames Valley Antique Dealers Association publishes a booklet of its members with their addresses and specialities. It can be obtained from:

The Secretary
Thames Valley Antique Dealers Association, The Old Cottage, Dorchester-on-Thames, Oxfordshire OX10 7HL (01865 341639)

There is an antique fair (the Oxford Fair) in October each year at St Edward's School, Oxford.

FACTFILE

Arts and Crafts

'High' art can be seen at:

Burghclere
Sandham Memorial Chapel

Oxford
Christ Church Picture Gallery
Museum of Modern Art

Watlington
Chiltern Sculpture Trail, any time

There are also some good fine art dealers, of which the following deserve special mention:

The Berkeley Gallery, 41–43 Lower Kings Road, Berkhamsted (01442 878300)

Chilterns Fine Art Gallery, 1 St Peter's Place, Wallingford (01491 826440)

Barry M. Keene Gallery, 12 Thameside, Henley-on-Thames (01491 577119)

Marlborough Studio Art Gallery, 4 Hughenden Yard, Marlborough (01672 514848)

There are numerous craft outlets throughout the area, particularly craft potters, maintaining a tradition which stretches back centuries. There are also art galleries in most of the larger towns in the area. Of particular note are:

Ardington Pottery, 15 Home Farm, School Road, Ardington (01235 833302)

Guy and Pip Perkins, 6 Green Street, Avebury (01672 539307)

Pewsey Vale Crafts, 1 Old Ford Court, Pewsey (01672 563823)

Wharfeside Craft Workshops, Devizes (01380 726051)

Cinemas and Theatres

There are cinemas in Aylesbury, Hemel Hempstead, Henley-on-Thames, Luton, Newbury, Oxford, Reading, Swindon and Wantage. There are theatres in Dunstable, Hemel Hempstead, High Wycombe, Luton, Oxford (The Old Fire Station and The Playhouse), Reading (The Hexagon and The Mill at Sonning), St Albans, Swindon and Wallingford.

Gardens and Parks

All sites at specified times unless otherwise stated

Ashdown
Ashdown Park, at any time

Avebury
Manor House Garden

Henley-on-Thames
Fawley Court

Lower Basildon
Basildon Park

Oxford
Botanic Gardens

Sonning Common
Herb Farm and Saxon Maze

Stonor
Stonor Park

Tring
Tring Park, at any time

Woolton Hill
Hollington Herb Garden

Historical Sites

Open at specified times unless otherwise stated

Archaeological Sites
Avebury
Silbury Hill, any time for viewing; the hill may not be climbed
Stone Circle, any time
Stone Avenue, any time
The Sanctuary, any time
West Kennet Long Barrow, any time
Windmill Hill, any time

Cholesbury
Iron Age hillfort, any time

Fyfield
Devil's Den, any time
Fyfield Down, any time

Little Wittenham
Castle Hill Iron Age hill-fort, Sinodun Hills, any time

Ridgeway
Barbury Castle Iron Age hill-fort, any time
Liddington Castle Iron Age hill-fort, any time
Uffington Castle Iron Age hill-fort, any time
Wayland's Smithy Neolithic Long Barrow, any time
Uffington White Horse, possible Iron Age hill figure, any time
Grim's Ditch, prehistoric rampart/ditch, any time
Scutchamer Knob, long barrow (?), any time

Battlefields

Bishops Canning
Roundway Down

Newbury
South-west of the town
North-west of the town, near Donnington Castle

Chalk Figures

Chilterns
Cross, Bledlow Ridge
Cross, Whiteleaf
Spire, Watlington Hill

Marlborough Downs
White Horse, Alton Barnes
White Horse, Broad Town
White Horse, Cherhill
White Horse, Hackpen Hill
White Horse, Pewsey
White Horse, Preshute
White Horse, Uffington

Historical Buildings

Ardington
Ardington House

Ashdown
Ashdown Park

Avebury
Great Barn
Manor House

Berkhamsted
Bridgewater Monument, can be viewed from the outside at any time

Burghclere
Highclere Castle
Sandham Memorial Chapel

Chalfont St Giles
Milton's Cottage

Chenies
Manor House

Ellesborough
Chequers, not open to the
public, but can be viewed from
the Ridgeway

Ewelme
Church, almshouses and school;
the church is open at any
reasonable time, the school and
almshouses may be viewed from
the outside only

Henley-on-Thames
Chantry House
Fawley Court

High Wycombe
Hughenden Manor

Hungerford
Littlecote House

Ivinghoe
Ford End Watermill
Pitstone Windmill

Jordans
Old Jordans Farm
Mayflower Barn
Friends' Meeting House

Lacey Green
Lacey Green Windmill; it can be
viewed from the outside at any
time

Medieval Sites
Berkhamsted
Castle, any time

Lower Basildon
Basildon Park

Mapledurham
Mapledurham House and Mill

Marlborough
The Merchant's House

Nuffield
Nuffield Place

Oxford
Bodleian Library
Sheldonian Theatre
The Colleges

Princes Risborough
Manor House

Rotherfield Greys
Grey's Court

Stoke Row
Maharajah's Well; it can be
viewed from the outside at any
time

Stonor
Stonor Park

West Wycombe
West Wycombe Park
Mausoleum

Wilton
Wilton Windmill; it can be viewed
from the outside at any time

Little Kimble
Cymbeline's Castle

Newbury
Donnington Castle, any time

Wallingford
Castle Gardens and Ruins

Ogbourne St Andrew
Snap, site of medieval village,
any time

Saxon Sites
Ashbury
Alfred's Castle Iron Age hill-fort,
possible site of Saxon battle,
any time

Ridgeway
Uffington White Horse, possible
Saxon hill figure, any time

Hotels and Restaurants

As major tourist areas, Oxford, the Chilterns and the chalk downlands
have a superb range of accommodation and restaurants from which
the visitor may chose. The choice is assisted by pamphlets issued by
the main and local Tourist Information Offices.

A sample of hotels and restaurants in the three main areas is
given below. The lists have been derived from personal experience or
recommendation, but the author and publisher cannot be held
responsible if your visit does not match your expectations. A simple
price guide – £ = inexpensive, ££ = moderate, £££ = expensive - is
given as a guide.

Hotels
The Chilterns
Danesfield House, Henley Road, Marlow (01628 891010)
Marvellous mansion set in 65 acres of landscaped gardens; excellent
restaurant (£££)

The Crown Hotel, High Street, Amersham Old Town (01494 721541)
16th century inn with Georgian façade; famously used as setting for
Four Weddings and a Funeral (£££)

Imperial Hotel, 25 Station Road, Henley-on-Thames (01491 578678)
Imposing Edwardian building close to the river and station (££)

George Thistle Hotel, High Street, Wallingford (01491 836665)
Close to the centre of town; a fine old coaching inn with a good
restaurant (££)

Belmont Hotel, 9/11 Priory Avenue, High Wycombe (01494 527046)
Close to the centre of the town, and the train and bus stations; no
restaurant (£)

Greyhound Inn, High Street, Chalfont St Peter (01753 883404)
14th century coaching inn with riverside gardens for the summer and
log fires for the winter (£)

The Downlands
Castle and Ball Hotel, High Street, Marlborough (01672 515201)
Elegant hotel positioned half-way along Marlborough's superb main
street (£££)

Bacon Arms Hotel, 10 Oxford Street, Newbury (01488 682512)
16th century coaching inn of great character, a short distance north
of the town centre (££)

Marshgate Cottage Hotel, Marsh Lane, Hungerford (01488 682307)
Small hotel in delightful country on the edge of the town; no
restaurant (£)

Oxford
Cotswold Lodge Hotel, 66A Banbury Road (01865 512121)
Lovely Victorian building in a quiet area just a few minutes walk from
the centre; excellent restaurant (£££)

Randolph Hotel, Beaumont Street (01865 247481)
The city's most famous hotel, opposite the Ashmolean Museum; two
fine restaurants (£££)

Old Black Horse Hotel, 102 St Clements (01865 244691)
Attractive 17th century building just across Magdalen Bridge (££)

Parklands Hotel, 100 Banbury Road (01865 554374)
Very conveniently positioned and with a good restaurant (££)

Cotswold House, 363 Banbury Road (01865 310558)
Close to the city centre; very comfortable, but no restaurant (£)

Westgate Hotel, 1 Botley Road (01865 726721)
A short walk from the city centre and also conveniently close to the train and bus stations (£)

Restaurants
The Chilterns
The Compleat Angler, Marlow Bridge, Marlow (01865 484444)
Beautiful, historic building beside the Thames; excellent food overlooking the river (£££)

The Copper Inn (Hotel and Restaurant), Church Road, Pangbourne (0118 984 2244)
Superb cooking and a lovely setting just a short step from the river (£££)

Gilbey's, Market Square, Amersham Old Town (01494 727242)
At the heart of old Amersham in a very pretty setting (££)

La Petite Auberge, Great Missenden (01494 865370)
Lovely little French restaurant with excellent menu, beautifully prepared (££)

Red Lion, High Street, Wendover (01235 850403)
Eat where Oliver Cromwell and Robert Louis Stevenson ate; excellent cooking (££)

Herveys, High Street, Wendover (01235 622257)
Simple, unpretentious, but very good (££)

Risboro Peking, Church Street, Princes Risborough (01844 342505)
Splendid Chinese restaurant in marvellous part-timbered building (££)

Milton's, opposite Milton's Cottage in Chalfont St Giles (01494 872172)
Delightful old English building serving typical Indian dishes; a terrific mix of cultures (££)

The Downlands
Coles, Kingsbury Street, Marlborough (01672 515004)
Relatively new restaurant just off the High Street; good varied menu (£££)

San Sicario, 28 High Street, Wallingford (01491 834078)
The best Italian restaurant in the area (££)

Raffles, 1 The Green, Aldbourne (01672 540700)
Good French cooking in a lovely setting at the heart of the village (££)

Madagascan Gin Palace, Inch's Yard, Newbury (01635 35491)
Interesting restaurant in a redeveloped, and charming, little square; all starters and main meals are the same price and the dishes are from all parts of the world (££)

Henley-on-Thames
There are several excellent (and pricey) places to eat in Henley-on-Thames, but there are also a couple of very good budget places too:

The Old Rope Walk Café, 20/22 Hart Street (01491 574595)
Occupying what was once the town's ropemakers, hence the long room and long garden; straightforward menu and good cooking in old world surroundings (£)

Francesco's, 8 Bell Street (01491 573706)
Pasta, pizzas and jacket potatoes in quaint little café (£)

Oxford
Bath Place, 4 Bath Place (01865 791812)
Award-winning French cooking in 17th century building close to the heart of the University (£££)

Restaurant Elizabeth, 82 St Aldates (01865 242230)
Arguably the finest place in town; high-class French cooking (£££)

Brown's, 5-11 Woodstock Road (01865 511995)
One of the most famous eating places in the city; varied menu and jazz pianist (££)

Fishers, 36/37 St Clements (01865 243003)
Oxford's only seafood restaurant, close to Magdalen Bridge (££)

Ashmolean Café, Ashmolean Museum, Beaumont Street
(01865 288183)
The perfect lunch spot (closes at 5pm); good quality home cooking (£)

The Nosebag, 6-8 St Michael's Street (01865 721033)
Irresistibly named, with good home cooking (£)

Leisure Activities

Boating
The information panel for Oxford gives details of punt hire on the Thames. For an even more leisurely trip, passenger boat services are available on the river; these are operated by Salter Brothers Ltd, whose main office is at Oxford's Folly Bridge. The passenger boats link the larger towns between Oxford and Staines. Boats can also be hired at Henley-on-Thames and Reading.

Canal Boats
The Kennet and Avon Canal is popular with narrow boat enthusiasts. British Waterways and the Kennet and Avon Canal Trust publish a leaflet on the canal with details of the locks, and companies from which boats can be hired for day or longer trips. There are also Canal Information Centres at Devizes and at Aldermaston Wharf, midway between Newbury and Reading.

The Grand Union Canal is also popular with narrow boat enthusiasts. Boats can be hired at Pitstone Wharf.

Cycling
The gently undulating country of the Downs and Chilterns is excellent for cycling and the local Tourist Information Offices have information on suggested routes. The Ridgeway National Trail from Avebury to Goring is a byway or bridleway throughout its length and is therefore open to cyclists. The Trail is deeply rutted in places and very difficult during or after very wet weather. If you intend to cycle, please make allowances for walkers, particularly older walkers. Modern mountain bikes are quiet and the walkers may not hear you approaching, sudden overtaking by one or more cyclists at speed contributing to the occasional animosity between walkers and mountain bikers.

Golf
Berkhamsted
Ashridge Golf Club, Little Gaddesden (01442 842244)
Berkhamsted Golf Club, The Common, Berkhamsted
(01442 865832/865851/863730)
Stocks Hotel, Golf and Country Club, Stocks Lane, Aldbury
(01442 851341)

Beaconsfield
Beaconsfield Golf Club, Seer Green
(01494 676545/676616/678180/681180)

Chalfont St Giles
Chorleywood Golf Club, Common Road, Chorleywood (01923 282009)
Harewood Downs Golf Club, Cokes Lane, Chalfont St Giles
(01494 762308/764102/762184)

Chesham
Chesham and Ley Hill Golf Club, Ley Hill (01494 784541)

Devizes
Erlestoke Sands Golf Club, Erlestoke
(01380 830300/831069/831027)
North Wilts Golf Club, Blackland, Bishops Canning
(01380 860330/860627)

Didcot
Hadden Hill Golf Course, Wallingford Road, Hadden Hill, North
Moreton (01235 510410)

Dunstable
Dunstable Down Golf Club, Whipsnade Road
(01582 604472/662806)
Whipsnade Park Golf Club, Studham Lane, Dagnall
(01442 842330/842331/842310/842090)

Henley-on-Thames
Aspect Park Golf Club, Remenham (01491 577562)
Badgemore Park Golf Club, Badgemore (01491 572206/573667)

High Wycombe
Hazlemere Golf and Country Club, Penn Road, Hazlemere
(01494 714722/718298/713914)
Wycombe Heights Golf Centre, Rayners Avenue, Loudwater
(01494 816686/812862/813185)

Ivinghoe
Ivinghoe Golf Club, Wellcroft Road, Ivinghoe (01296 668696)

FACTFILE

Marlborough
Marlborough Golf Club, The Common, Marlborough
(01672 512493/512147)
Ogbourne Downs Golf Club, Ogbourne St George
(01672 841217/841327/841362)

Newbury
Deanwood Park Golf Course, Stockcross (01635 48772)
Donnington Valley Golf Course, Donnington (01635 581000)
Newbury and Crookham Golf Club, Greenham Common, Thatcham
(01635 40035)
Newbury Golf Centre, Newbury Racecourse (01635 551464)

Nuffield
Huntercombe Golf Club, Huntercombe, Nuffield (10491 641207)

Oxford
North Oxford Golf Club, Banbury Road, Oxford
(01865 554415/554924)
Oxford Golf Centre (Binsey Driving Range), Binsey Lane, Oxford
(01865 721592)
Southfield Golf Club, Hill Top Road, Oxford
(01865 242158/242656/248944)

Pewsey
Upavon Golf Club, RAF Upavon (01908 630281)

Princes Risborough
Whiteleaf Golf Club, Princes Risborough (01844 343097)

Reading
Mapledurham Golf Club, Chazey Heath, Mapledurham
(0118 946 3353)
Reading Golf Club, Emmer Green, Reading
(0118 947 2909/947 6115)
Richfield Driving Range, Richfield Avenue, Reading (0118 957 3700)

Streatley
Goring and Streatley Golf Club, Streatley
(01491 873229/872688/873715/875224)

Wendover
Ellesborough Golf Club, Butlers Cross
(01296 622114/622375/623126)

Horse Riding

Hardly surprisingly in an area renowned for its racehorses, the Downs and Chilterns are ideal riding country with several riding schools and stabling opportunities. The Ridgeway National Trail is a byway or bridleway from Avebury to Goring and can therefore be ridden along its length. Tourist Information Offices have details of riding schools and stables.

Sports Centres

There are sports centres in Chalfont St George, Chesham, Devizes, Didcot, Dunstable, Hatfield, Hemel Hempstead, Henley-on-Thames, High Wycombe, Hungerford, Luton, Marlborough, Marlow, Newbury, Oxford, Pangbourne, Reading, St Albans, Swindon, Watford and Welwyn Garden City.

Swimming Pools

There are swimming pools in most of the sports centres in the towns mentioned above. There are also pools in Ringshall and Princes Risborough

Walking

The Marlborough and Berkshire Downs and Chilterns are superb walking country, most of the area being flat or gently undulating.

The Ridgeway National Trail traverses the chalk ridge from end to end, a total of 137km (85 miles). There are several other long-distance paths which also make use of the upland chalk. The London Countryway crosses the Chilterns near West Wycombe/Great Missenden, while the Thames Path follows the river through Goring Gap. The Ickieild Way is a continuation of the ancient ridge path from Ivinghoe Beacon, and the North Bucks Way touches the Chilterns near Great Kimble.

Those keen on canal walking can follow the towpath of the Kennet and Avon Canal through the Vale of Pewsey or that of the Wendover Arm of the Grand Union.

In addition, there are numerous short waymarked trails through the Chiltern woodlands, and local Tourist Information Offices have leaflets on short walks in their areas.

Museums

Agricultural
Pitstone
Pitstone Green Farm

Historical
Amersham
Amersham Museum

Avebury
Alexander Keiller Museum
Great Barn/Rural Life Museum

Chalfont St Giles
Chiltern Open Air Museum

Devizes
Devizes Museum

High Wycombe
Local History and Chair Museum

Newbury
West Berkshire Museum

Oxford
Ashmolean Museum
Museum of the History of
Science
Museum of Oxford
Oxford Story
Pitt-Rivers Museum of Ethnology
(and Annexe)

Reading
Museum of English Rural Life
Museum of Reading

Wallingford
Wallingford Museum

Wantage
Vale and Downland Museum

Industrial
Crofton
Canal Beam Engine

Ivinghoe
Ford End Watermill
Pitstone Windmill

Lacey Green
Lacey Green Windmill

Oxford
Museum of the History of
Science

Reading
Blake's Lock Museum

Wilton
Wilton Windmill

Wroughton
Science Museum Annexe,
Wroughton Airfield

Literary
Chalfont St Giles
Milton's Cottage

Uffington
Tom Brown's School Museum

Model
Long Wittenham
Pendon Museum

Musical Instruments
Oxford
Bate Collection of Musical
Instruments

Natural History

Oxford
University Museum

Tring
Walter Rothschild Zoological
Museum

Sporting

Henley-on-Thames
River and Rowing Museum

Transport

Devizes
Kennet and Avon Canal Centre

Didcot
Didcot Railway Centre

Reading
Blake's Lock Museum

Nature Reserves

Inkpen
Inkpen Common

Little Wittenham
Little Wittenham Nature Reserve

Stokenchurch
Aston Rowant National Nature
Reserve

Thatcham
Discovery Centre

Wendover
Wendover Woods

Other Visitor Sites

Beaconsfield
Bekonscot Model Village

Booker
Blue Max Movie Museum

Fingest
Chiltern Valley Winery and
Brewery

Oxford
Morrells Brewery

Terrick
Chiltern Brewery

West Wycombe
West Wycombe Caves

Whipsnade
Tree Cathedral, any time

Wildlife

Andover
Finkley Down Farm Park

Bucklebury
Bucklebury Farm Park

Chesham
Allsorts Farm

Great Gaddesden
Longford Children's Farm

Hampstead Norreys
Wyld Court Rainforest
Conservation Centre

Horsleys Green
Gibbons Farm Rare Breeds

Ipsden
Wellplace Zoo

Lower Basildon
Beale Park

Ship End
Woodside Wild Fowl Park

Speen
The Home of Rest for Horses

Stoke Mandeville
Bucks Goat Centre

Thatcham
Thatcham Discovery Centre

Whipsnade
Whipsnade Wild Animal Park

Index

INDEX

INDEX